United Methodist

God's
Healing
Community

God's Healing Community

FRANK BATEMAN STANGER

Abingdon
Nashville

GOD'S HEALING COMMUNITY

Library of Congress Cataloging in Publication Data

Stanger, Frank Bateman.
  God's healing community.
  Bibliography: p.
  1. Faith-cure. I. Title.
BT732.5.S73   615'.852   78-8017

ISBN 0-687-15332-8

**MANUFACTURED BY THE PARTHENON PRESS AT
NASHVILLE, TENNESSEE, UNITED STATES OF AMERICA**

DEDICATED

to my wife

MARDELLE

*who from the first moment that I met her
has been
a minister of healing to me
through her wise counseling
her life of faith and grace
her unending love
her exemplary relationship
as a helpmate all along the way
her constant insistence upon
the good and the beautiful and
the true*

CONTENTS

WHY I AM WRITING

This is a book about the possibility of a person experiencing healing and the responsibility of the church to engage in a ministry of healing. It is the result both of my personal healing and of more than a quarter of a century's study of and participation in a healing ministry following such a healing.

During all these years I have been impressed by several facts: (1) the growing interest in healing on the part of Christians, (2) the increasing emphasis upon the activity of healing in the ministry of the church, and (3) the noticeable successes in the church's ministry of healing. All this has led to a deepening conviction of the indissoluble relationship between salvation and wholeness.

During these years, I have wanted to write a book that would both present my spiritual convictions about the church's ministry of healing and would be sufficiently informative of the whole field to enable interested persons to understand, to seek, and to participate. I am in touch with persons regularly who are deeply concerned and who are desirous of such information and guidance.

This volume is intended to deal with the basic elements in the understanding of the nature of healing and of the practice of a ministry of healing. I send this book forth with the fervent prayer that every person who reads it will be led into an experience of personal wholeness through the power of the Great Physician. I also pray that every local congregation everywhere will become an active participant in the church's ministry of healing. Then will come to pass in our day the fulfillment of Jesus Christ's great commission to his first disciples: Go—teach, preach, heal!

I want to express my deep appreciation to my friends in First United Methodist Church, Collingswood, New Jersey, who supported me when I pioneered in a regular healing ministry there; to the many readers of my healing column in *The Herald* who have encouraged me with their appreciative words; to the members of my healing classes at Asbury Theological Seminary who through the years have inspired me in my pursuit and presentation of healing truth and many of whom have gone forth from the seminary to inaugurate healing ministries in their own churches; to my former secretary, Helyn Johnson, who typed the original manuscript, always in her inimitable gracious manner and in her painstaking workmanship; and to Sylvia Culver, who now serves as my secretary and who has carried on the task of extensive revisions with her editorial finesse and efficient skills.

F.B.S.

HOW IT ALL BEGAN

It was a hot July evening more than a quarter of a century ago. I vividly recall standing in the kitchen of our parsonage home, partly watching my wife perform the after-dinner chores and partly reflecting upon my recent illness that had forced me to give up my ministerial duties, at least for the time being. Just five months before I had been appointed the pastor of this thriving suburban church of nearly fifteen hundred members. Seemingly my ministry in this church had begun well, and I was anticipating with a high sense of privilege and delight an unfolding ministry in a church that was warmly evangelical and intensely evangelistic. But my nerves got the better of me, my emotional reserves became depleted, and after a very distressing series of attempts to carry on my demanding duties, I gave up and sought the help of a medical doctor who had been a high school classmate of mine.

I remember well this particular July evening, for it was the fourteenth day after my doctor friend said I would feel much better in two weeks. But I didn't feel better; I actually felt worse. The emotional aspects of my illness manifested themselves in a wave of almost despair, and I recall saying to my wife: "I'm finished; I guess my ministry is over."

Unknowingly, but immediately, my wife became a minister of healing to me. Every Christian is called to be a minister of healing to others. She reached out, took hold of my elbow, and confidently asserted: "You're not finished; you are just beginning."

However feebly, my spark of hope responded to her flame of faith, and that moment became the turning point in the process of my healing. I was out of the pulpit for ten weeks and spent a portion of the time on a trip abroad. All the while the healing process proceeded beautifully, and I was healed completely. In a vital and life-changing way, I experienced the healing power of God.

The crucial test of my faith came on the Sunday morning when I returned to my pulpit. A large congregation greeted me in an attitude of prayer and expectancy. I had battled all week the thought that I might not make it. This was the very pulpit I had failed in before. Would I succeed now? Was I actually healed? Was I adequate again?

I have thought many times since those days that this was my Jerusalem experience. E. Stanley Jones wrote concerning the appropriateness of the early Christians receiving the baptism of the Holy Spirit on the Day of Pentecost in Jerusalem. It became their assurance that it is possible to succeed in the very place where they had previously failed. It was in Jerusalem that Peter had denied his Lord, that Judas betrayed Jesus, and that the other disciples went into hiding because of their fears. But Pentecost made everything different. Now they were filled with a divine power; they were made adequate to be and do what God intended, and failure turned to success. Pentecost meant succeeding in the very place where they had failed before. Because of my healing, the past twenty-six years have been the most creative and productive of my entire life and ministry.

From the time of my healing I have been a student in the field of healing and most of that time a participant in the church's ministry of healing. Previously I had had but little contact with that particular area. I do not recall ever hearing about the matter during the time I spent in theological seminaries. If it was mentioned then, it certainly made no impression upon me. I do recall, however, the first time in my personal study that the dynamic truth of Christ's purpose to bring wholeness to the total person was impressed upon me. I was reading E. Stanley Jones' book *Is the Kingdom of God Realism?* Some years later I had the personal delight of having Dr. Jones autograph that very book. Above his signature he wrote, "Jesus is Lord! Of the body—of Everything."

My in-depth study of healing and the relation of the Christian faith to it began with such books as *Psychology,*

Religion, and Healing by Leslie D. Weatherhead, *Religion, Healing and Health* by James Van Buskirk, *The Gospel of Healing* by A. B. Simpson, and the writings of such participants in the healing ministry as Elsie Salmon, Rebecca Beard, and Agnes Sanford. During succeeding months, the list of available books increased significantly, and I discovered a wealth of healing materials at hand. It is interesting to note that such healing literature has increased phenomenally during the past two decades. My study also included contemporary periodicals and reports of the news media, and I began a rather extensive healing clipping file.

After nearly a year of such intensive study, certain convictions about the relationship between the Christian faith and healing began to take definite shape in my thinking. These original convictions, five in number, which have deepened in intensity through the years, will be discussed in detail in chapter 4. These convictions formed the basis of a satisfying theology of healing that has emerged for me during this more than a quarter of a century in which I have been active in the field.

Soon I felt the inward compulsion to prepare a series of sermons based upon these convictions and to share with the members of my church my newly discovered insights in this area of healing, which at that time was a largely unknown field to most church members. As the original series of sermons in my local church progressed, interest on the part of the congregation increased tremendously. Before the series was over, the church was packed on Sunday morning to hear what was being said in this field which was new to most people. At the close of the last sermon in the series, I made the announcement that beginning that afternoon there would be regular healing services, at least monthly, as long as I was the minister. And there were—for nearly seven years.

It was in this way that my healing ministry began. I thank God that it has never ceased. I have participated in a host of healing seminars, conferences, and missions in the United

States and Canada. I have shared with ministers of many denominations in prayers for the sick and in services of anointing and the laying on of hands. I have written in the field of healing for periodicals regularly across the years. For fifteen years I have taught a course entitled "Healing and the Christian Faith" in a graduate school of theology. I am in correspondence frequently with pastors who are conducting regular healing ministries in their churches and, of course, there are ever-present opportunities for personal ministries of healing.

Three Observations About the Contemporary Interest in Healing

1. The contemporary interest in healing is the inevitable expression of an agelong and universal concern for healing. From earliest times persons have been intent in their search for healing. Disease is at least as old as the Fall of Man.

Use of Nonphysical Healing Methods. A study of primitive religions reveals that as long as five thousand years ago health and disease were believed to depend on states of the mind. It was assumed that a mental state of reverence for, and fear of, a god brought health while indifference or hostility to the deity resulted in disease. Hence, the use of nonphysical methods to combat disease is very ancient. Astrologers, sorcerers, and magicians in ancient Egypt, Babylonia, Chaldea, Arabia, Judea, Greece, and Rome believed in the efficacy of charms and incantations, of strange concoctions, and of religous rites for the purposes of healing.

In the ancient world the god of healing was Asclepius. The two great centers of his worship were Rome and Epidaurus. Epidaurus has been called the Lourdes of the ancient world. Sufferers came to these temples and spent the night there in the darkness. The emblem of Asclepius is the snake. Accordingly, tame and harmless snakes were let loose in the dormitories. When they touched the people lying there, the people thought that it was the touch of the god, and they were healed.

Medical Science. Hippocrates, born about 460 B.C., is generally honored as the Father of Medicine. He believed that diseases have natural causes and should be treated accordingly. In his medical practice he was cautious, trusting chiefly to the operations of nature and to the effects of diet and regimen. As to surgery, he followed the maxim that what cannot be cured by medicine must be cured by fire. He classified the fluids or humors of the body as blood, phlegm, black bile, and yellow bile; the right combination of which resulted in health, and any disturbance of which caused disease.

In the Greco-Roman world, into which Jesus was born, the doctor was held in high esteem. It is from Greece that we get the famous Hippocratic oath, the oath taken originally by Greek doctors before they entered upon the practice of medicine and the oath that to this day governs medical ethics and practice.

The story of medicine and its amazing discoveries and achievements during the Christian centuries is a dramatic revelation of the universal concern for healing. Every student of the church's ministry of healing ought to peruse at least a general outline of the history of medicine.

Healing Ministries in the Christian Church. The healing ministry of Jesus Christ, as recorded in the New Testament gospel records, and the regular ministry of healing in the early church, as revealed in both canonical and noncanonical books, are highly significant confirmations of the unrelenting concern of persons for healing. In subsequent lessons we shall look in more detail at both the healing ministries of Jesus and of the early church.

The healing ministry was prominent in the Christian church until the beginning of the fourth century. With the rapid institutionalization of the church after its adoption as the official religion of the empire, the emphasis upon healing under church auspices became less prominent. In fact, it may be said that as far as the regular ministries of the church are concerned, the healing ministry of the church waned for more than a thousand years. Nevertheless, during all of this period that we call the Middle Ages, the church was not left without a healing witness in every century. There were those Christian leaders in each of the centuries who emphasized the forgotten ministry of healing and by their participation in it helped to restore it to the normal life of the church. But they never accomplished their hoped-for purpose on a universal level.

The Reformation, with its emphasis upon the Holy Scriptures, made possible a climate more conducive to both belief in and practice of healing within the church. The Reformation emphasis was so largely theological in its focus, however, that healing activities were limited largely to personal experiences. It is interesting to note in passing that each of the reformers bore witness to some kind of experience in relation to healing.

Let it also be kept in mind that the healing emphasis at least in theory has never been entirely lost at any time in the long history of Roman Catholicism. The Roman Catholic Church has long recognized both material and supernatural powers in healing. The student of healing soon becomes aware of the phenomenon of such a healing center as Lourdes.

2. There is an unusual revival of interest on the part of the church in the healing ministry. Recent decades have witnessed the rise of cults, most of which have a healing emphasis, and the formation of smaller sects within Protestant Christianity that also have included healing in their basic tenets and practices. A large number of the small denominations that have come on the American scene during the past century have had an active healing emphasis.

Recent years have witnessed the revitalization of the healing emphasis in the older, larger Protestant denominations. Leaders in the healing ministry and healing movements are now to be found in most of these denominations. Church commissions have been formed to investigate and report on the healing ministry of the church. A large number of local churches now carry on regular healing ministries. An increasing number of books in the field of healing are being authored by concerned scholars and church members. There is a growing interest in healing within many theological seminaries.

Let me venture five answers in response to the question, Why is there an unusual contemporary interest in the church's ministry of healing?

   a. The focus upon the possibility of the healing of the person is an antidote to the alarming and increasing trend of depersonalization in the contemporary age, particularly in industrial and scientific pursuits.

   b. There is a growing concern for the total person. Man is clearly seen as a unity. The influence of the component parts of the person upon one another is increasingly manifest. Wholeness is no longer compartmentalized; it relates to the total person. Such an emphasis upon wholeness is manifest in the behavioral sciences and medical science as well as in theology.

   c. Within the church there is a quickened concern about its total ministry. The contemporary church is rediscovering that it must minister according to the pattern of Jesus' ministry and that of the early church—preaching, teaching, healing.

   d. There is concerned and diligent investigation of the spiritual impetus that undergirds the growing ministries of so many active healing groups both within and outside the Protestant Christian framework.

   e. There is a growing sensitivity to the total needs of people in the contemporary age. There has never been a time when so many people needed some kind of healing. Hosts of people are burdened, bored, tired, nervous, physically ill, emotionally upset, and lacking in spiritual wholeness. There is conscientious concern that persons everywhere discover authentic healing for their many ills.

3. It is of special significance that the medical profession is committed to treating the whole person. Medical science no longer isolates man's body from the rest of his personality. A person is viewed as a whole person. Paul Tournier, eminent Swiss doctor and author, speaks of this as "the medicine of the person."

Doctors are recognizing increasingly the relation between mind and emotions and body and the effect of each upon the others. Some months ago a syndicated column by a well-known doctor had articles on the spirit of Thanksgiving and the spirit of Christmas and the effect of such a spirit upon a person's health.

Consultations on medicine and theology are being held. The American Medical Society has created a department of medicine and religion. There is an intensified emphasis upon the work of chaplains in hospitals and healing institutions. There is a growing cooperation between doctors and clergy in the treatment of illness.

Some Basic Convictions

Naturally, after more than a quarter of a century of study and activity, I have some basic convictions about the church's ministry of healing. Let me share them with you, as a background for our more detailed studies in the pages that follow:

1. Healing is one of the ministries that Jesus Christ has committed to his church. When the church fails to engage in a healing ministry, it is not being fully obedient to its Lord. The Great Commission is binding upon the church: Go teach—go preach—go heal!

Alan Whanger, a former missionary/surgeon in Rhodesia, was a pioneer in the conduct of healing services in mission hospitals and is now active in the practice of psychiatry in the United States. Dr. Whanger shared with me his conviction that the church should engage in a healing ministry primarily because our Lord commands us to do so. We are to obey his commands in spite of the results. He remarked that the church does not stop evangelizing because everyone is not converted. Nor should the church refuse to participate in a healing ministry because everyone is not healed.

2. God wills wholeness for the total person. It is a pagan rather than a Christian concept to believe that God hands out suffering and permits evil on the assumption these are essential ingredients in the formation of spiritual character and the fulfillment of spiritual ministry. Jesus Christ did not divide a person into body and soul, but he saw each one as a whole person. He came to save persons, not just souls. Sickness of the mind and body was part of the kingdom of Satan that Christ came to destroy!

The intellectual problems involved in such a conviction do not lessen with the passing of the years. Many are not healed. A young minister dies of cancer. A mother is stricken fatally in her early thirties. A promising business executive is paralyzed as a result of an injury inflicted by another. A freak accident wipes out an entire family.

But the conviction deepens—the divine ideal is wholeness. And if the healing should be postponed until after death, then the healing of eternity becomes the ultimate guarantee of wholeness in spite of the perversions, distortions, and fatalities of sinful mortality.

3. There is no solitary and exclusive method of healing. There must be no divisive issue between so-called material and spiritual methods of healing. As we shall see later in our study, the healing ministry of the church employs every legitimate healing method. All healing, by whatever method it is accomplished, is of God.

4. Healing is not achieved through any magical means or haphazard methods, through any hocus-pocus or sleight of

hand. The laws of healing have been revealed, and the healing steps are relevant for every person seeking healing. In the final analysis God's healing power flows in response to authentic prayer. Later in our study an entire chapter is devoted to the healing steps and another to healing prayer.

5. There are no ultimate failures in the church's ministry of healing. Even in those cases when physical or emotional healing is not complete, the highest healing is always a person's right relationship to the living Christ and the wholeness of spirit and the peace that results from such a relationship.

6. Every Christian is called to be a minister of healing. Those who have experienced the healing power of the risen Christ and whose regenerated hearts are set on fire by the Holy Spirit are already in the healing ministry, whether they recognize it or not.

Every Christian has a healing ministry. God may have given special talents to some—the general practitioner, the surgeon, the psychiatrist, the minister, the social worker—but each Christian, regardless of vocation, has a role in the healing community. Every Christian is caught up in the mending process of love and forgiveness and prayer. The ministry of healing, thus, becomes a part of the universal priesthood of all believers.

QUESTIONS FOR REFLECTION

1. What contacts have you had with healing or a healing ministry?
2. Is concern for wholeness a sign of normality within a person? What about the obverse: Is preoccupation with thoughts of illness an evidence of the lack of normality?
3. Is your church a healing church?
4. Can you recall something that a doctor has said to you about the relationship of mind and emotions and spiritual states to physical health?
5. Should Christians try to console one another by saying that everything that happens is the will of God?
6. Do you know persons in whom a miracle of healing has taken place? Have you ever experienced such a healing?

WHAT DO WE MEAN BY HEALING?

Healing has been labeled in various ways: faith healing, divine healing, Christian healing, spiritual healing. Even though these are all valid terms and express an aspect of the total truth, I believe that each of the terms is too restrictive in relation to the total healing ministry. Therefore, we should seek a proper designation.

A Proper Designation

Faith healing usually implies the activity of a faith healer. Too frequently the focus is centered upon a person who appears to have a particular gift of healing. The result is that a person's faith becomes dependent upon his personal proximity to such a person and upon the faith healer's activity on his behalf. Even though faith is an essential in the healing process, healing can be hindered when such faith is in any way dependent upon a human channel of God's healing power rather than upon God himself who is the source of all healing.

Divine healing is too general a term. All healing is of God and thus should be spoken of as divine. The danger in the use of this term is that we tend to fall back on the arbitrary sovereignty of God in relation to the release of his healing power and as a result often bypass the opportunities of a concentrated and continuing healing ministry. Certainly we may believe that God's healing power is released in response to intercessory prayer as well as the result of his own arbitrary sovereignty.

The term *Christian healing,* although it implies Jesus Christ as the Great Physician, may give the wrong impression that only Christians can be healed through a healing ministry. The record of healing proves the contrary. The possibility of healing is a universal reality and transcends religious boundaries. In fairness to the healing ministries of many of us, however, it must be said that our prior concern is always that the person seeking healing first of all come into a right relationship to God through Jesus Christ.

The term *spiritual healing* is often used popularly, though I think mistakenly, to refer to the total ministry of the church in relation to healing. Technically spiritual healing is healing solely through spiritual means, rather than through any physical or psychological methods. Spiritual healing is healing through faith, prayer, spiritual disciplines, and the dominance of spiritual values in one's quest for wholeness. Actually, spiritual healing means reliance upon meditation instead of medication, aspiration rather than aspirin, consecration more than a clinic, surrender rather than surgery, prayer instead of prescriptions.

Certainly there is an overlapping in all of this. Spiritual methods must be actively related to the use of all physical and psychological methods of healing. But healing is not limited to spiritual methods alone.

I have come to the conviction that the proper designation of what we are talking about is *the church's ministry of healing.* Since the church is primarily concerned about wholeness, it is interested in every legitimate healing method as means to achieve such wholeness.

The church participates in many ministries—the ministry of worship, of proclamation, of education, of evangelism, of fellowship, of social concern and action. From its institution the church has also been assigned a ministry of healing. William Barclay writes: "Preaching, teaching, healing—that was the threefold pattern of the ministry of Jesus. Healing was an inseparable part of his work and of the pattern of the work of his apostles." Jesus' great commission to his church is threefold: Go teach—go preach—go heal.

An Adequate Definition

We need also an adequate definition of healing. Many excellent definitions of healing have been given. Let us consider several before discussing the one that will be considered basic in this entire series of lessons.

The following insights are offered by Bernard Martin, a minister in Geneva, Switzerland, and a longtime leader in the church's ministry of healing:

> The healing of man is a liberation from physical, mental, and spiritual shackles which prevent him from reaching the full maturity of a man destined for eternal life.
>
> To heal a man includes more than protecting him from destruction. It is also to provide him with the possibility of pursuing his path, to lead him to a progressive blossoming of his person, to return to him the capability of living.
>
> Sickness is everything which, in one way or another, hinders a man in his path toward the full humanity of Jesus Christ. The healed man therefore is a man in whom the obstacles to the development of his true nature have been eliminated. To be healed means more than to recover the life that one led before falling ill. To be healed means to live normally in every area of one's life.[1]

James D. Van Buskirk, M.D., longtime medical missionary, wrote: "Healing is the removing of all obstacles to the natural healing powers resident in us, through the power of God."[2] From the pen of T. F. Davey, M.D., comes this descriptive definition of healing:

> Healing is directed to man's need for wholeness. Health in the Christian understanding is a continuous and victorious encounter with the powers that deny the existence and goodness of God. It is participation with Christ in an invasion of the realm of evil in which final victory lies beyond death, but the power of that victory is known now in the gift of the life-giving Spirit.[3]

Evelyn Underhill, twentieth-century mystic and spiritual practitioner, spoke of healing as the restoration to true normality, mending the breaches in our humanity and making us again what God intends us to be. The life-giving Spirit is ever at work, counteracting the substandard existence created by all disease of soul or body and restoring fullness of life.

One of the significant church-related studies of healing in recent years was made by a special commission on religion and health appointed by the Protestant Episcopal Church. In its official report (1964), healing is described as "an endeavor to achieve wholeness of mind, body and spirit within the larger context of a vital Christian faith."

The name and work of Morton T. Kelsey, professor at Notre Dame University, in the contemporary healing ministry is universally recognized. Dr. Kelsey speaks of healing as "rescuing men from the domination of the enemy." Canon Noel Waring describes spiritual healing as "God's loving action upon all and every part of our nature."

Against the background of the above definitions and descriptive statements, let me share the most adequate definition of healing that I have discovered. It was given by the late Leslie D. Weatherhead, eminent British clergyman and a pioneer in the contemporary concern for the church's ministry of healing.

> By healing, then, is meant the process of restoring the broken harmony which prevents personality, at any point of body, mind, or spirit, from its perfect functioning in its relevant environment; the body in the material world; the mind in the realm of true ideas and the spirit in its relationship with God.[4]

This particular definition will be considered basic and formulative in all the studies in this volume.

Basic Truths About the Meaning of Healing

A study of these definitions reveal some basic truths about healing. First, healing relates to normalcy within the person. Healing has as its objective the making possible of the normal functioning of the person on the highest level of being. Weatherhead speaks of "restoring the broken harmony"; Martin speaks of "a liberation from shackles which prevent maturity," "a return to the capability of living," "to live normally in every area of one's life"; Underhill speaks of "making us again what God intends us to be."

In the second place, healing relates to every aspect of the human personality—body, mind, and spirit. Healing is concerned with wholeness for the total person. Sometimes the basic need of a person is for physical healing. At other times the basic need is mental and emotional. Again the basic need is often spiritual. Perhaps there are fundamental needs in more than one area of human personality. Or there may be the need for the harmonious working of all the component parts of the human personality.

The church's ministry of healing rests fundamentally upon the nature of men and women, as created by God in his own image. We have been created as a unity. The basic components of our nature—spirit, mind, and body—are distinct entities but interrelated, and together they comprise a personality that ideally is characterized by unity. We fulfill the potential of creation only as the various parts of our personalities work in harmonious balance and affect each other constructively.

Jesus healed persons rather than merely curing diseases. The individual is truly healed in so far as he recovers the possibility of the maturity of his entire person. The healed person is restored and set once again within his true destiny. Healing means wholeness, and such wholeness is dependent upon the Holy Spirit's integration of one's total being—body, mind, and spirit.

There is a third truth: Healing is usually a process. Weatherhead calls it "the process of restoring the broken harmony." Nevertheless, this emphasis upon process is not meant to exclude either instantaneous healings or instantaneous acts of faith that initiate the process of healing.

Finally, healing is always purposeful. Healing is never effected for purposes of self-display or even primarily for verbal witnessing. Healing is never to be sought merely as another miracle that the omnipotent God gives a person to toss about. Rather healing always relates to the perfect functioning of the person. The New Testament concept of "perfect" includes the idea of divine purposefulness. Healing makes possible not only divinely intended activity in furtherance of the kingdom of Jesus Christ but also maturity of being in Christ.

QUESTIONS FOR REFLECTION

1. What was your idea of healing when you began reading this book? Was it limited to the physical area of one's being, or did it also include the mental/emotional/spiritual areas?

2. Do you believe that all healing is of God? Do you believe that healing is just as divine when it is effected through natural and scientific means as when it is miraculous?

3. Do Christians have special privileges above other persons to ask God for healing?

4. What definition of healing given in this chapter is most helpful to you?

5. How do you react to the statement: Healing is usually a process?

6. When Jesus Christ touched a person, how extensive did he intend his healing to be?

WHAT DOES THE BIBLE SAY?

Basic to our understanding of the healing ministry of the church is at least a general acquaintance with what the Bible says about healing. It soon becomes evident to a student of the Holy Scriptures that the Bible is a book of healing and that its pages are replete with stories of healings.

Old Testament

Naturally we begin with the Old Testament. In the Old Testament God revealed himself as Healer. One of the Hebrew names by which God is called is Jehovah-rapha— "The Lord who heals." God gave this revelation of himself to the Israelites after he saw their plight in Egypt and was purposing to deliver them. God reiterated his healing power as he promised his people, "I will take sickness away from the midst of you" (Exod. 23:20-25 RSV).

Throughout the Old Testament, healing prayers were addressed to God. For illustration: "Heal her, O God, I beseech thee" (Num. 12:13 RSV). "O Lord, heal me" (Ps. 6:2 RSV). "Heal me, O Lord, and I shall be healed" (Jer. 17:14 RSV). Such prayers are grounded in faith in a God who heals. (Study Job 2:5; Ps. 103:2-3; Isa. 53:4-5.)

"The Lord who heals" also manifested himself in prescribing laws of health, which when observed become the basic antidotes to sickness and disease. These laws of health that were divinely given may be summarized under six main headings: (a) the law of sanitation (see Exod. 29:14), (b) the law of cleansing (see Lev. 15), (c) the law of isolation (see Num. 5:1-14), (d) the law of dietetics (see Lev. 11), (e) the law of personal disciplines (see Num. 6), (f) the law of rest (see Exod. 20:8-11; Lev. 25).

In his book *None of These Diseases,* S. I. McMillen, M.D., documents the relationship between the observance of the divinely given laws of health and the fulfillment of the divine promises in Exodus 15:26 and 23:25—"I will put none of these diseases upon you," "I will take sickness away from the midst of you." Later the psalmist testified to the fulfillment of the earlier divine promise: "There was not one feeble person among their tribes" (Ps. 105:37).

Among the personal healings recorded in the Old Testament are the following:

The healing of Job	Job 42:1-17
The healing of Abimelech's household	Genesis 20:17
Miriam healed of leprosy	Numbers 12:1-16
Healing from the serpents' stings	Numbers 21:4-9
Child restored from death	I Kings 17:17-24
Shunammite's son raised	II Kings 4:18-37
Healing of Naaman	II Kings 5:1-14
Healing of Hezekiah	II Kings 20:1-11
	Isaiah 38
The preservation of Daniel's health in spite of his diet	Daniel 1:10-16

Perhaps this is a good place to remark that there is a reference to healing in the Apocrypha (Ecclus. 38:1-14).

There are many psalms that have a healing focus and provide valued healing insights. Psalm 6 pictures the destructive effects of negative emotions upon a person's health. Psalm 23 pictures the very opposite: the therapeutic effects of positive emotions upon the total personality.

Psalm 32 presents the imperative of confession and repentance for one's total well-being. Guilt manifests itself even in one's body. Health is impossible apart from forgiveness.

Psalm 38 and 39 are the prayers of a person who is suffering because of his sin. The psalmist appeals to God for forgiveness and the restoration of wholeness.

Psalm 51 is an impassioned prayer for spiritual healing. "Be merciful to me, O God. . . . Wipe away my sins! Wash away all my evil and make me clean from my sin!" (Ps. 51:1-2 TEV).

In Psalm 62 a sufferer from a severe illness waits for God's healing help with inner calm and trustful expectancy.

Psalms 91 and 103 speak of God's healing power for his chosen people in sweeping terms: "He will keep you safe from all . . . deadly diseases. You need not fear . . . the plagues that strike in the dark" (91:3, 5 TEV). "He . . . heals all my diseases" (103:3 TEV).

The student of the psalms discovers repeated references to the confidence of the people in the healing power of God. There was always the conviction that when God sent his word, healing resulted (107:20), and that the true response to God's healing was always that of gratitude and worship and obedience (116).

Certain truths emerge from a study of healing in the Old Testament:

1. A state of good health was pictured as the ideal situation. Nevertheless, the realization of such a state of good health was sometimes impeded by the erroneous Hebrew concept that good health is usually the arbitrary reward of goodness, and sickness is the arbitrary judgment for sin.

The Hebrew dogma that all sickness and suffering is the punishment of God is certainly not the total Christian perspective in the matter. It is true that in a moral universe, sickness and suffering often results from a person's sin and failure to obey the laws of God. In this regard God often offered counsel on how to be kept from sickness and suffering. But there is also much suffering and sickness for which an individual is not responsible and certainly through which he is not being punished morally. The full Christian perspective is realized only as one understands that wholeness is the will of God for every person.

2. God was continually manifesting himself as the One who heals. Whenever healing became evident in Old Testament times it was considered a divine work, and praise was offered to God for it.

3. There was a growing awareness in the Old Testament that wholeness related to the total person. It was always believed that such wholeness began with harmony with God. Consequently, prayer for mental and physical healing often included prayers for spiritual purging. The Bible is unwavering in its revelation that a right relationship to God is always the ultimate objective.

New Testament

As we move to the New Testament, we begin with the life and ministry of Jesus Christ. The Old Testament had predicted that the coming Messiah would perform a ministry of healing. In the beautiful fifty-third chapter of his recorded prophecy, Isaiah describes him as "a man of pains, and acquainted with diseases," as the One who bore our diseases and carried our pains (Isa. 53:3-5 Jewish Version). The New American Bible translates Isaiah 53:5 in this way: "Upon him is the chastisement that makes us whole." Little wonder is it that one of the familiar titles of Jesus Christ when he ministered in the flesh was that of Great Physician.

When Jesus appeared, he was a personal demonstration of good health and wholeness. We read in the New Testament Scriptures that he was tempted, he became hungry, tired, discouraged, lonely, sad; but never are we told he was ever sick. And the portrait of him wherever it is found is one of emotional wholeness and of perfect spiritual harmony with his Father.

Jesus' concern for the human body was in line with the best religious thought of his day. He carried on an extensive ministry of healing. In the Gospels, there are records of at least twenty-six healing miracles that Jesus performed upon individuals. There are numerous other references to multiple healings in the ministry of Jesus. A listing of these healings proves helpful in our study:

Individual Healings by Jesus	Matthew	Mark	Luke	John
Nobleman's son				4:46-54
Unclean spirit		1:21-28	4:31-37	
Simon's mother-in-law	8:14-15	1:29-31	4:38-39	
A leper	8:1-4	1:40-45	5:12-16	
Paralytic carried by four	9:1-8	2:1-12	5:17-26	
Sick man at the pool				5:2-18
Withered hand	12:9-14	3:1-6	6:6-11	
Centurion's servant	8:5-13		7:2-10	
Widow's son raised			7:11-17	
Demoniac(s) at Gadara	8:28-34	5:1-20	8:26-36	
Issue of blood	9:20-22	5:25-34	8:43-48	
Jairus' daughter raised	9:18-26	5:21-43	8:40-56	
Two blind men	9:27-31			
Dumb, devil-possessed	9:32-34			
Daughter of woman of Canaan	15:21-28	7:24-30		
Deaf, speech impediment		7:32-37		
Blind man of Bethsaida		8:22-26		
Epileptic boy	17:14-21	9:14-29	9:37-42	
Man born blind				9:1-14
Man blind, deaf, possessed	12:22-30		11:14-26	
Woman bent double			13:10-17	
Man with dropsy			14:1-6	
Raising of Lazarus				11:1-44
Ten lepers			17:11-19	
Blind Bartimaeus	20:29-34	10:46-52	18:35-43	
Malchus' ear			22:50-51	

Multiple healings in the Ministry of Jesus	Matthew	Mark	Luke	John
Crowd at Peter's door	8:16-17	1:32-34	4:40-41	
Casting out of devils		1:39	(Acts 10:38)	
Crowds after leper healed			5:14-16	
Crowd near Capernaum	12:15-21	3:7-12	6:17-19	
Answering John's question	11:2-6		7:18-23	
Women healed of evil spirits, including Mary Magdalene			8:2	
Before feeding the five thousand	14:13-14		9:11	
At Gennesaret	14:34-36	6:53-55		
Before feeding four thousand	15:29-31			
Crowds beyond the Jordan	19:1-2			
Blind and lame in temple	21:14			
Some sick of Nazareth	13:53-58	6:1-6		
All kinds of sickness	4:23	6:56		
Every sickness and disease	9:35			
Instructions of Jesus and promises to Believers	10:7-8	6:7 16:14-20	9:1-2 10:8-9	
Sending of Twelve	10:1, 7-8	6:7-13	9:1-6	
Sending of Seventy			10:1-20	
Jesus' witness to his healing works			13:32	
Perfect eternal healing		(Revelation 21:4)		

A medical classification of Jesus' healing miracles shows that he healed the following known ailments: fever, malaria, leprosy, congenital blindness, Parkinson's disease, nephritis, arthritis, fibroids of the uterus or functional hemorrhage, epilepsy, deafness, blindness, crippledness, and insanity. And certainly Jesus must have also encountered such conditions as the neuroses that are associated with such symptoms as fear, anxiety, insomnia, nervousness, palpitation, heart disorder, indigestion, excitement, and depression.

When Jesus sent forth his disciples, he instructed them, among other things, to heal the sick. "And when he had called unto him his twelve disciples, he gave them power against unclean spirits, to cast them out, and to heal all manner of sickness and all manner of disease" (Matt. 10:1).

Many significant summary truths evolve from a study of the healing ministry of Jesus:

1. Jesus devoted much of his ministry to works of healing. Luke, the physician, has more references to his healing work than any other gospel writer.

2. When we study the gospel records it becomes evident that Christ's healing work was on a different level than that of mere human science. We stand in the presence of One who lived on a higher spiritual plane than we normally penetrate, and spiritual energies of immense power were at his disposal.

3. Christ's healing miracles are not the same as mere psychological cures. Scientific research and discoveries are not adequate to release the energies used by Christ.

4. Jesus Christ did not break any established cosmic laws in the effecting of his healing miracles. Weatherhead defines a miracle as "a law-abiding event by which God accomplishes his redemptive purposes through the release of energies which belong to a plane of being higher than any with which we are normally familiar." Another has said, "Miracles are not contrary to nature, but only contrary to what we know about nature."

5. Jesus' primary motivation in his healing ministry was that of compassion. Because he loved people, he wanted them to

become whole in every part of their being. He never did any of his work for the sake of self-display.

6. The real object of Christ's healing miracles was spiritual and redemptive: through the inflow of God's power to infuse God's truth into human minds, to pour God's love into human hearts, to bring persons into a right relationship to God.

7. It was inevitable that the healing miracles of Christ's ministry should become authentic signs of the Kingdom he came to establish. As he commissioned the disciples he declared: "Heal the sick . . . and say unto them, The kingdom of God is come nigh unto you" (Luke 10:9).

The Early Church

As the earthly ministry of Jesus was drawing to a close, He told his disciples that "he that believeth on me, the works that I do shall he do also; and greater works than these shall he do" (John 14:12). In fulfillment of the divine promise and in obedience to the divine command, healing became a regular ministry in the early Christian church.

The following is a record of both individual and multiple healings in the book of Acts:

Individual Healings by the Apostles

Healing of the lame man from birth	Acts 3:1-10
Paul regains his sight	9:12, 17, 18
Healing of Aeneas the paralytic	9:32-35
Raising of Dorcas from the dead	9:36-42
Healing of the crippled man at Lystra	14:8-10
Raising of Paul who had been left as dead after being stoned	14:19, 20
Healing of a slave girl with the spirit of divination	16:16-18
Raising of Eutychus from death after falling from upper story window	20:7-12
Paul kept from harmful effects of deadly snake bite	28:3-6
Healing of father of Publius	28:8

Multiple Healings by the Apostles

The New Testament writers often related the health of the body to the spiritual life of the individual. A wholesome spiritual life contributed to health of body and mind. The apostle John wrote solicitously: "I wish above all things that thou mayest prosper and be in health, even as thy soul prospereth" (III John 2). On the other hand, an improper use of the means of grace can result in sickness. Paul, in writing about an irreverent participation at the time of the Lord's Supper, says: "For this cause many are weak and sickly among you" (I Cor. 11:30).

In his epistle, James gives interesting instructions to the sick concerning prayers for healing:

> Is any among you afflicted? let him pray. Is any merry? let him sing psalms. Is any sick among you? let him call for the elders of the church; and let them pray over him, anointing him with oil in the name of the Lord: and the prayer of faith shall save the sick, and the Lord shall raise him up; and if he have committed sins, they shall be forgiven him. (5:13-15)

A study of the early church brings into prominence several major emphases in relation to healing:

1. Healing was a regular ministry in the early church. It was the continuation of Jesus' healing works. It was the fulfillment of Christ's great commission: Go—teach, preach, heal. The apostles possessed and exercised an authority to heal in the name of Jesus.

2. A part of the witness of the early church was the declaration of the divine source of healing power. Healing was

in the name of Jesus, the divine Son of God (Acts 3:6, 16; 19:11-13). The healing ministry of the church was always an occasion of the Spirit's presence in personal joyfulness and in corporate evangelism and growth (Acts 2:43, 46-47; 3:8; 4:21; 5:14; 8:6-8).

3. The healing ministry in the early church was a dramatic evidence of the aliveness of Jesus Christ. The Resurrected One was in their midst, performing his mighty works. Even their enemies were powerless to stop the onrushing spiritual tide of this new movement that affirmed and worshiped Jesus as Lord.

The Gift of Healing

Our study of healing in the early church would be incomplete without some mention of the gift of healing. In I Corinthians 12, Paul declares that the gift of healing is one of the gifts of the Holy Spirit that has been given to the church. He writes:

> But the manifestation of the Spirit is given to every man to profit withal. For to one is given by the Spirit the word of wisdom; to another the word of knowledge by the same Spirit; to another faith by the same Spirit; to another the gifts of healing by the same Spirit; to another the working of miracles; to another prophecy; to another discerning of spirits; to another divers kinds of tongues; to another the interpretation of tongues: But all these worketh that one and the selfsame Spirit, dividing to every man severally as he will. (I Cor. 12:7-11)

The specific gift of healing is to be viewed in the light of certain truths concerning spiritual gifts in general: (a) The gifts are charismatic in nature. They are gifts of God's grace. (b) The validity of the gifts is based on Christ's redemptive triumph. (c) The gifts have a common source—the Holy Spirit. (d) There is a distinction between gifts of the Spirit and the Gift of the Spirit. The Gift of the Spirit is the fullness of the

Spirit for every believer. The gifts of the Spirit are bestowed upon divinely selected, Spirit-filled individuals for specialized ministries. (e) There is a variety of gifts. (f) The distribution of the gifts is in accord with divine wisdom. (g) The gifts are to be used for the good of all.

Any discussion of the gift of healing raises an inevitable question: Has this spiritual gift of healing, so prominently used in the early church, ever been withdrawn?

Even though there are those who say that the gift of healing has been withdrawn, there does not seem to be any internal or external evidence to support their claim. Rather it appears that the gift of healing remains the possession of the church as the body of believers. Even in New Testament times when the gift of healing was evident in the activities of individual Christians, it was given for their use for the common good. Thus it is logical to believe that the gift of healing now belongs to the whole body of believers, and the contemporary church under divine inspiration is to carry on an active ministry of healing.

QUESTIONS FOR REFLECTION

1. What do you think is the connection between one's relationship to God and one's health? Is good health the reward of righteousness? Is sickness the consequence of evil in one's life?

2. Why did Jesus devote so much time to a ministry of healing?

3. Select several of the healing miracles of Jesus and study them with the following questions in mind:

    a. What was the cause of the person's illness?

    b. What were the various attitudes toward a possible cure?

    c. Who took the initiative in seeking a cure?

    d. What was the place of faith in effecting a cure?

    e. What was the procedure followed in the healing?

    f. What were the evidences of the healing?

    g. What were the responses to the healing?

    h. Why do you think Jesus effected this particular healing?

    i. What does the particular healing say to us today about the healing ministry of the church?

4. Why did the early church devote so much time to a ministry of healing?

5. What similarities do you discover between the healing ministry of Jesus Christ and that of the apostles in the early Church:

    a. In taking the initiative toward the healing?

    b. In speaking hopeful healing words?

    c. In the use of particular healing methods?

    d. In calling upon the person being healed for his or her cooperation?

6. How do you react to the idea that in our day perhaps the gift of healing is given primarily to the church as a group of believers, rather than merely to individuals?

THE RELATIONSHIP BETWEEN THE CHRISTIAN FAITH AND HEALING

For some reason "theology" is often a word that persons are afraid of. Such a fear is evidence that one understands neither the actual meaning of theology nor the makeup of one's own mind and spirit. Actually, theology is one's reflection upon God, a study of what is thought and said about him, and a sincere attempt to have some kind of understanding of his nature and his active relation to the persons and world that he has created. In a very real sense, each thinking person is a theologian. Of course, very few of us are professional theologians, but we are all theologizing when we sincerely seek to know more about God and to understand in as practical manner as possible the ways in which he relates himself to us.

The Need for a Theology of Healing

Theology is needed to impel one to continuing dedicated spiritual being and doing. Even though we may not always be quick to identify such a causal relationship, it takes a theology of prayer for us to pray, a theology of love for us to love and serve, a theology of spiritual experience for us to worship and witness, a theology of stewardship for us to give in the New Testament sense, a theology of the church for us to be good church members, a theology of truth and holiness for us to be ethical.

Contemporary theology is in desperate need of an adequate theology of healing. The distance between the theological world and the experience of healing is pointed out by Morton T. Kelsey in his volume *Healing and Christianity:*

> Christian theology does not seem to be looking at the facts concerning healing. Instead, one has the distinct impression of a foregone conclusion. The most comprehensive survey of recent theology, John Macquarries' *Twentieth Century Religious*

Thought makes this quite clear. Healing is simply overlooked today. Of the hundred and fifty theologians discussed in that book, not one emphasizes the effect of man's religious life on his mental and physical health, as do the more perceptive psychiatrists and students of psychosomatic medicine. Few of these religious thinkers, in fact, even bother with arguments against healing.[5]

Just so, both the contemporary healing movement and the contemporary church need an adequate theology of healing. This is imperative to undergird the phenomenal resurgence of healing activity and experience and to motivate and sustain the church in the practice of the healing ministry. Such a theology of healing needs to become a part of our basic Christian convictions.

One's basic attitude toward healing, whether one believes or disbelieves or just waits dispassionately to be convinced one way or other, is actually dependent upon one's theology. One's experience of healing is dependent upon one's theology. What God can do depends upon what a person thinks he can do. What a person thinks God can do depends upon what he or she believes God is like.

Participation in a ministry of healing is also dependent upon one's theology. We must become channels through which God's healing power can flow. Clear channels of God's power require Christlikeness in spirit and life. It is our Christian theology that interprets for us the true meaning of Christlikeness. In a very real sense, our views of God, of miracles, of prayer, of faith, of salvation, influence our healing activities.

A theology of healing, therefore, has to do with those aspects of theological truth that we believe reveal God as supportive of and active in the total healing process. Actually there is not a theology of Christian healing per se. Such an isolated theology would tend to make healing an end in itself, and this could pervert God's purposes into self-centered action. A theology of healing grows out of basic Christian theology.

A theology of healing builds upon our confidence in the authenticity of the divine revelation in the Holy Scriptures and particularly as this revelation exposes God's desire for and activity in relation to wholeness within the creature and the creation. A theology of healing assumes our acceptance of a scriptural view of God as Creator, of the divinely designed nature of human creation, and of the activity of the divine Creator in the restoration of his fallen creation.

A satisfying theology of healing emerges for us because of our theology of creation, which views men and women as created in the image of God; our theology of the kingdom of God, which thus shows the divine purpose to be the fulfillment of the divine will within the creation; our theology of the church as a healing community; and our theology of the endless life, which calls for the final and perfect restoration of humankind.

Early Personal Insights into a Theology of Healing

My personal theology of healing began to emerge early in my studies in the area. During that first year of personal healing and intensive research I became increasingly convinced of the vital relationship between the Christian faith and healing. I began to understand this relationship in five areas. These were the convictions I shared with the members of my congregation during my first series of sermons on healing. These are the initial convictions that have deepened with the years. Today they are even more compelling than during that meaningful period when my healing ministry was beginning to emerge.

Let me now share what I have discovered to be the fivefold relationship between the Christian faith and healing.

The Gospel of Health

To begin with, the Christian faith inspires healthy living, and this is the best prevention of disease. Just suppose an individual from his early life really lived the Christian way—would not healthy living result in most instances and much sickness be avoided?

James Van Buskirk has written of nine characteristics of the Christian way of life, all of which contribute to health.

1. Christianity teaches and encourages the proper care of the body.
2. The Christian religion enforces the virtue of honest work, which has a definite therapeutic value.
3. The Christian faith promotes recreation and relaxation.
4. Christianity encourages a person to turn from himself and to rest in the Lord.
5. The Christian faith encourages Christian worship, which has a significant therapeutic effect.
6. Christianity encourages the study of the Bible, thus allowing its constructive power to operate upon the personality.
7. The Christian gospel offers faith as the only antidote to fear.
8. The gospel of Jesus Christ frees the human personality from the devastating burden of guilt.
9. Jesus Christ always says "forgive," "love one another."[6]

I have a longtime minister friend who is now a distinguished professor in a theological seminary. I first became acquainted with him when he was a youth in one of the churches that I pastored. I have kept in touch with him across the years, and he has always encouraged me by his interest in the church's ministry of healing. On one occasion he invited me to participate in a healing conference being held for the ministers of the district on which he was serving in one of the south-western states. In fact, it was a sort of pioneer conference in relation to healing in that particular area.

I spoke to the ministers on the subject that is the title of this chapter. After my message, my friend was quick to comment on this matter of the Christian faith enforcing good health. I shall always remember his words:

You know me well. You know the way I lived as a youth. I was strong and rugged and thought I could eat what I wanted and live the way I wanted to. I really thought it was more important to be always active in Christian work than to take care of my body. But I have learned the hard way. I wish I had understood earlier the importance of observing the laws of health. Friend, wherever you go, keep preaching and teaching the gospel of health.

Spiritual Aids to Physical/Psychological Healing

A second relationship between the Christian faith and healing is that the Christian faith is able to aid healing through physical and psychological methods by the creation of the proper mental, emotional, and spiritual attitudes within the patient. Just as healing through physical methods is impeded by wrong mental, emotional, and spiritual attitudes, it is aided by right attitudes. This is clearly demonstrated in what is commonly known as the will to live.

Negatively considered, there are case records of what are called psychological deaths. There are patients who lose interest in life, and feeling that there is nothing worth living for, they succumb to the first illness that comes along. I read in the daily press the other day of a lady who months before had set July 4, 1977, as the date of her death. This became the focus and obsession of her life. And she died on July 4, 1977.

Even when death does not result, the process of physical or mental recovery is impeded drastically and prolonged by wrong attitudes toward life. A doctor once told of the surprisingly slow recovery of a patient after a mild attack of influenza. Even though there was no physical cause for her continuing debility, she continued to have no appetite, a poor pulse, and to look unfit. Finally, it was discovered that the reason she was failing to recover normally was because she did not want to recover. If she recovered, she knew she would have to return to a job that was causing her much unhappiness.

Positively speaking, it is this will to live that is often the deciding factor between death and recovery. An anesthetist remarked that patients who go to the operating table with a confident faith in God take less anesthetic, recover from it more easily and with far less of the usual distressing aftereffects.

In *Pity My Simplicity*, Paul Sangster tells of the saintly Henry Venn who lay dying for so long a time when his death had seemed so imminent days before. On one occasion the doctor told his daughter Jane: "Madam, your father would have died a fortnight ago if it had not been for joy at dying."[7]

Cooperation of Medical Science and the Church's Ministry of Healing

To make our study complete, there is a third relationship between faith and healing that should be mentioned. There have been times when the church's ministry of healing and medical science have joined hands to effect a healing, each contributing something to the healing that the other could not.

There is a record of a young boy in South Africa who needed a brain operation but was subject to blackouts. The brain surgeon in Johannesburg said that he could not operate until the boy had been free of blackouts for six months. In desperation the parents took their son to Elsie Salmon, the wife of a Methodist minister who has had a remarkable ministry of healing. After eight months, the boy had experienced no blackouts. They returned him to the surgeon in Johannesburg. The operation was performed. It was one of the earliest operations on record where they removed a sphere of the brain. The operation was a success, and the young man became one of the outstanding artists in South Africa.

Now what had happened? The church's ministry of healing did something and medical science did something to make possible the healing. Each made a contribution that the other did not make. Certainly there is being confirmed in our day the validity of this intensely cooperative relationship between medical science and the church's ministry of healing.

Healing of Functional Illnesses

The fourth relationship between the Christian faith and healing is discovered in the very areas in which most people live. The Christian faith is able to direct the healing of all those functional illnesses that have been caused by wrong mental, emotional, or spiritual attitudes.

There is a difference between an organic or structural illness and a functional illness. In an organic or structural illness something is wrong with the nature of the organ or body structure itself. A functional illness is one in which there is nothing inherently wrong, but an organ or a bodily structure is malfunctioning. And what is the cause of such malfunction? The answer is clear: wrong mental attitudes or negative emotions or improper spiritual relationships or a combination of these within a person. Doctors estimate that 80 percent of all sickness is functional in nature. This is what is known as psychosomatic illness.

How devastating is the effect of wrong mental attitudes, negative emotions, and improper spiritual relationships upon the total person. Every negative emotion, except the normal expression of grief, is destructive. Such things as fear, anxiety, ill will, guilt, inferiority, and negativism are destructive in their effect upon the human personality. E. Stanley Jones quotes the following statistics in his writings:

Blaine E. McLaughlen, director of psychiatry at Women's Medical College, Philadelphia, says that 60 to 85 percent of all patients in doctors' offices have psychosomatic complaints. Dr. McLaughlen says that 99 percent of all headaches, 75 percent of all gastric upsets, 75 percent of skin diseases, and 85 percent of all asthma cases are psychosomatic in nature.

According to Dr. Jones, a doctor who attended the medical needs of a General Motors plant in a certain city said: "Seventy-five percent of the executives of this plant have gastric ulcers due to the pressures upon them to succeed or be replaced."

Karl Menninger says: "Guilt changes the physical structure of the body and makes the person more susceptible to disease." As a healing counselor, I spent an entire year trying to help a young man get over the ravaging effects of guilt in his life, and particularly upon his physical body, by accepting the forgiveness of Jesus Christ. At last the victory came! He was both forgiven and healed!

John W. Keyes, a heart specialist of the Henry Ford Hospital in Detroit, Michigan, declared that some heart disease may be imaginary, brought on by the patient's fears and his doctor's words or attitudes. Dr. Keyes explained: "The patients may have symptoms ranging from chest pains to dizziness, from fatigue to palpitations. Once symptoms of this type have occurred, they of themselves can produce a vicious cycle of anxiety which convinces the patient that heart disease is actually present."

I recall a business executive talking to me about being healed from the horrible fears that bound him continually. His daily life was haunted by all kinds of fears, and no longer could he function normally either at business or in the home.

I remember a young minister who talked with me during a healing conference. He wanted to share with me that at last, through our discussion of psychosomatic illness, he had discovered the reason for his vomiting every time before preaching in his church. It was a feeling of inadequacy, a sense of the fear of failure that took possession of his bodily processes.

I think of another young minister who in the midst of a healing seminar remarked that for the first time in his life he had come to realize the destructive power of negative thinking upon his health and ministry. He confessed that he had often wondered what was wrong. Now he knew that the wrong kind of thoughts had produced "dis-ease" in every part of his being. He rejoiced that constructive thinking was being offered him as a beautiful therapy.

The only effective way to deal with functional illnesses is to deal with their basic causes. The mind must be disciplined away from wrong mental attitudes and into the direction of positive, constructive, authentic thinking. The heart must be filled with new spiritual energies. Negative emotions must be replaced by positive emotions. The guilt-ridden must find true forgiveness. Fear must be replaced by faith, anxiety by confidence. Ill will and resentments must give way to genuine love. A sense of hostility must be replaced by an attitude of acceptance in Christ. Inferiority attitudes must be supplanted by a sense of adequacy through spiritual resources. Negativism must be rejected as an anti-Christian attitude. A sense of futility must be replaced by a sense of divine purpose for one's life. All relationships must be reconciled in conformity with the teachings and example of Jesus Christ. All of this is possible only through the power of Jesus Christ actively at work within a spiritually responsive and fully cooperative person.

Healing by Direct Activity of God

The final aspect of the relationship between the Christian faith and healing is healing by the direct activity of God apart from the use of intermediary psychological or physical methods. When we speak of healing by the direct activity of God, we refer to God intervening directly in a person's experience, apart from all recognizable human sources of remedy and cure, bringing to the individual healing that is clearly demonstrable at the place of the mind or soul or body, in a combination of any two of these areas of human personality, or in a combination of all three areas.

Human experience offers irrefutable evidence of the healing power of God after human skill has proved ineffective and after physical and psychological methods have exhausted themselves.

I would never have known my father if God had not healed him through his direct touch during the dreaded influenza epidemic that followed World War I. The Christian world would never have been enriched by the saintly lives and faithful ministries of persons like E. Stanley Jones, Albert Cliffe, and Catherine Marshall LeSourd had not God intervened with his healing touch into their hopeless circumstances of illness.

After I studied the life of Dwight Eisenhower, I was convinced that we would never have shared in his leadership had not a direct healing taken place during his early boyhood. The family doctor said that his injured leg needed to be amputated. Dwight made one of his brothers promise that he would never allow it to happen. His godly parents went to prayer. The infection was stopped, and the leg mended. Dwight Eisenhower would never have completed his vocational pilgrimage from West Point to the White House, by way of the battlefields of Europe, apart from two healthy legs.

As I move among people speaking about the healing ministry of the church, there are repeated testimonies to God's miraculous healing power shared with me. If you have ears that are attuned, you will also hear such witnessing to the Great Physician.

QUESTIONS FOR REFLECTION

1. What are your ideas of God? How do these relate to God as Healer?
2. Are you convinced that good health is a Christian responsibility?
3. Have modern psychiatry and psychology been able to improve upon the teachings of Jesus concerning the healthy way to live?
4. Have your thoughts/emotions ever made you sick?
5. Are you learning how to discipline your mental/emotional life?
    a. Are you learning how to deal with destructive states and emotions? With guilt? Fear and anxiety? Ill will? Inferiority? Negativism?
    b. Are you trying to cultivate positive thoughts and emotions within yourself?
6. How can the local church encourage greater cooperation between its own ministry of healing and medical science in its various branches?

A SATISFYING THEOLOGY OF HEALING

A theology of healing that has become satisfying to me intellectually and that is adequate to support my participation in the church's ministry of healing has developed from these basic convictions discussed in the previous chapter. The relationship between the Christian faith and healing has been the foundation upon which my theology of healing has been built.

It needs to be noted also that my developing theology of healing has had some decisive existential undertones. There has never been a time when so many people needed some kind of healing. People lack radiance. Individuals seem burdened and bored. In the faces and attitudes of people there is evidence of insecurity and fear. This is due to the need for some kind of inward healing.

Everywhere people are unusually tired. One of the major types of chronic fatigue is psychological. Such fatigue has been described as "an illness due to being caught in a trap." E. Stanley Jones lists nine psychological and spiritual causes of tiredness: self-centeredness, boredom, worry, fear, inferiority feelings, resentments, indecisions, oversensitivity, inner guilts.[8] All such causes require healing within the person.

Consider all the nervous illness in the world. Nervous maladies are probably responsible for more mental and physical suffering than any other category of disease. And what about the vast amount of mental sickness? It is estimated that at least one in every ten Americans is suffering from a mental or emotional disorder. Mental sickness is becoming a major problem in American industry. Emotional problems figure prominently in the staggering loss in billions of dollars that American industry suffers each year in absenteeism, employee turnover, alcoholism, industrial accidents, and lowered productivity caused by friction between workers.

Consider also the prevalence of physical illness. Hospitals

everywhere are crowded. The sickness costs among the American people are staggering.

And how tragic is the spiritual sickness everywhere evident. There is a declining sense of respect for authority, and acts of lawlessness are increasing phenomenally. The old immorality has become the new morality. Persons are alienated from God and separated from their neighbors. Hostility is too often the mood of interpersonal relationships. Nothing other than the balm of Gilead, effected at the cross of Christ, can provide the needed healing.

It is my conviction, and it certainly has theological dimensions, that God does not stand unmoved and inactive in the presence of all this vast amount of suffering, this unfathomable need for healing, everywhere in his world. He is continually offering "life and life more abundantly." His healing ministries are a contemporary expression of his boundless, redeeming grace.

But now let me speak in more specific detail about the other tenets in my theology of healing. These have been worked out as a result of my continuing study and active participation in the church's ministry of healing across the years. These tenets are but confirmation and amplification of my basic theological conviction of the vital relationship between the Christian faith and healing. I share four such tenets that contain valid theological implications for a healing ministry.

The Divine Creation of Persons

The human creature, in the varied aspects and manifestations of his person, as the creation of God, has intrinsic and eternal value. First of all, the total person has intrinsic value. The Holy Scriptures reveal persons as created in the image of God—a rational, moral, spiritual image. God passed his highly favorable verdict upon his creation. "And God saw everything that he had made, and behold, it was very good" (Genesis 1:31 RSV). The history of Christian ethics reveals that personality has always been regarded as the most precious part of God's creation.

The incarnation of Jesus Christ reveals the intrinsic worth of the total person. "Jesus increased in wisdom and stature, and in favour with God and man" (Luke 2:52). Throughout his ministry, Jesus was concerned about the hurts of the total person—physical, mental, emotional, spiritual—and their healing.

In a more particular sense the human body has intrinsic value. The Old Testament reveals this in its picture of the divine creation, in its revelation of the Levitical laws to safeguard health, and its relating physical and spiritual health in its concept of salvation.

The incarnate Christ appeared in a human body and "dwelt among us" (John 1:14 RSV). The ministry of the incarnate Christ revealed the concern of Jesus Christ for the human body. His miracles of healing upon the body were so numerous that he was known as the Great Physician.

The New Testament Scriptures speak of the body being redeemed (I Cor. 6:20); justified, sanctified, washed (v. 11); being a member of Christ (v. 15); being indwelt by the Holy Spirit (v. 19); belonging to God (v. 19); and ultimately being raised up (v. 14). Little wonder is it that the apostle Paul exhorts us to glorify God in our bodies (v. 20).

Addison H. Leitch summarizes the significance of the human creature in these words:

> Man is akin to the earth, akin to the lower creation. He is dust and to the dust he returns. At the same time he is of the spirit of God himself. As man he is both soul and body, and the "inbreathing" of God seems to mean that every cell of his physical being is thus inbreathed. . . . You cannot touch his body at any point where you do not find him "inspired."[9]

This truth is being recognized increasingly by contemporary man. The October 11, 1974, issue of *Evangelical Newsletter* quotes the results of a survey of forty thousand *Psychology*

Today readers in these words: "God has moved. The bearded Jehovah in the clouds has, for many, become the mysterious force in the gut, or an immanence infesting the whole body/mind."

God Wills Wholeness

God wills wholeness for his creatures. I do not believe that God wills sin or sickness or accident or affliction. Illness is not the will of God. Sickness is not necessary for the development of character or for the fulfillment of God's will. We must disabuse our minds of any wrong supposition that carrying one's cross means the acceptance of illness as the will of God. In the New Testament sense taking up one's cross, bearing one's cross, is always a voluntary act that a person chooses to do. On the other hand, having illness thrust upon a person is always involuntary, in so far as normal personalities are concerned.

God wills that every person be whole in every aspect of his being and that such wholeness in body, in mind, and in soul be harmonized in a total personality wholeness. In *The Lord Is Our Healer,* Emily Gardiner Neal emphatically declares that disease does not emanate from God but from Satan and that there is no incurable disease in God's sight. Paul Tournier, noted Swiss physician, while admitting that disease can be fruitful declares: "It can also destroy all man's values, and as a doctor I shall not cease to try and snatch its victims from it."[10]

Let me share in a summary manner the reasons why I believe that God wills wholeness.

1. God's purpose for his creatures as expressed in the original creation is seen to be that of wholeness. The original creation was perfect. The Scriptures tell us that God said it was "good, very good." The way that God created man originally must have been the way he wanted him to be always. Thus, any lack of wholeness in a person is the result of sin or some evil force rather than the purpose of God.

2. Speaking of the creation of the human body, God has made us with built-in, automatic powers of healing. Within us are the natural processes of recuperation and restoration which are active in all healing. Frank G. Slaughter describes this built-in process of healing:

> In the body, for example, the necessity for police may arise whenever bacteria enter and infection threatens. As soon as this happens, the police department goes into action, white blood cells are rushed to the spot, and reserve cells are called into action from the bone marrow. Blood vessels are widened so that more blood can be brought to the danger zone. A complex physical and chemical reaction begins whereby substances to combat the bacterial invasion are manufactured quickly—potent bacteria fighters called "antibodies." Actually all this takes place a long time before we become conscious that anything untoward has happened. Only when swelling, pain and local redness and heat from increased blood flow attract our attention do we become conscious that something unusual has been going on. Automatically the body's defense system sets all these forces in motion to combat the enemy infection.[11]

After quoting the above in his book *God Wants You to Be Well*, Laurence H. Blackburn concludes:

> Why did God make us with fifty billion white blood cells or leucocytes, as they are called? Is it not because God is truly on the side of health, not of sickness? It is in the divine plan and purpose that we be at our physical best.[12]

3. The earliest known comprehensive set of health laws is found in the Old Testament. Instruction is given concerning personal cleanliness (Lev. 11:28; 15:5); purity of the water supply (Lev. 11:32-36); proper disposal of body wastes (Deut. 23:12-14); quick burial of the dead (Deut. 21:23); use of clean food (Lev. 11; 19:5-8; Deut. 14:21); and isolation of persons contaminated by the dead (Lev. 5:2), by unclean discharges (Lev. 5:3; 15:1-13), and by skin diseases (Lev. 13). Terminal

disinfection was provided for both people and things that were contaminated (Lev. 14:34-48; 15:1-13). Isolation of women following childbirth (Lev. 12:1-8) was an effective method in that day of preventing childbed fever. Venereal diseases were effectively controlled by the promulgation of sexual morality (Exod. 20:14; Lev. 18:1-20). Provision was made for the enforcement of these laws by the function of a kind of health officer, the priest (Lev. 13, 14). The divine ideal of wholeness for his human creatures shines clearly through these biblically revealed prescriptions for good health.

4. The Old Testament prophets had insights into God's purposeful wholeness. At times in the Old Testament writings the terms "salvation" and "health" are used almost interchangeably.

5. The perfect health of Jesus Christ, the incarnate Son of God, is a revelation of the glory of humanity expressed through the possibility of wholeness. Even though Jesus was subject to temptation, fatigue, disappointment, and the like, there is no record of his ever being sick. On the other hand, he fought sickness in every form.

Jesus was a balanced person in every respect. He is our model of wholeness. Marvin Mayers, former professor of anthropology at Wheaton College, remarked about Jesus' seamless robe being symbolic of the wholeness of his person and life-style. As a whole person he related to people with a redemptive desire that they become whole in the development of their total lives.

One function of the incarnation of Christ is to reveal the glory of humanity, a revelation of what humanity could have been if sin had not entered. In Jesus we see God living life as God would have lived it if God had been a man.

6. Consider also the healing ministry of Jesus. The healing acts of Jesus were the divine message that he had come to make people whole. He called his healings works rather than miracles, for they were the normal thing for him to do. Jesus declared: "I am come that they might have life, and have it

more abundantly." The gospel records reveal dramatically that whenever Jesus Christ touched human life, he restored wholeness.

7. The Divine Commission to the church reveals God's will that persons should be whole. Jesus commissioned his disciples to teach and preach and heal. As we have noted, preaching, teaching, and healing comprised the threefold pattern of the ministry of Jesus and of the early church.

The gift of healing was one of the gifts of the Holy Spirit imparted to the early church. Was this mere mockery, or was it rather a charismatic confirmation of the divine intention that persons should be whole? Students of apostolic and post-apostolic times affirm that the early church had a regular ministry of healing.

8. Are we willing to write off the significant influences of the church's ministry of healing through the centuries as outside the will of God? What about hospitals under Christian auspices? What about medical missions? What about deeply committed medical researchers and practicing physicians? What about miracles of healing through the centuries? What about the phenomenal rise of the church's ministry of healing in our day?

9. Finally, the contemporary medical emphasis upon what Tournier calls "the medicine of the person" is a scientific confirmation of the divine intention of wholeness. Physicians know that the total person must be healed if any part of the person is to be healed fully. The human being is all of one piece, and physical and spiritual attitudes cannot be treated independently. Either men and women are treated in their wholeness as human beings, or they are not really treated. Today's education of the future physician emphasizes personal and social values as well as scientific knowledge and abilities.

It would appear that a person's faith and prayer in seeking healing rests upon this basic conviction that God wills wholeness. When a member of my family was engaged in a demanding process of personal healing, a process that at times was agonizing and sometimes almost self-defeating, she would say to me over and over again: "But I keep on hoping and praying because you tell me that God doesn't want me to be the way I am."

It is just as evident that a church's ministry of healing must build upon this same foundational truth that God wills wholeness. Unless God wills wholeness, what right have we to seek it for ourselves or others?

Relationship Between Salvation and Wholeness

Salvation and wholeness are intimately related; you cannot separate them. I think of Jesus' words in which he relates "health" and "wholeness" and "salvation." For illustration:

> Heal the sick . . . and say unto them, The kingdom of God is come nigh unto you. (Luke 10:9. See also Matt. 10:7-8.)
> The blind receive their sight, and the lame walk, the lepers are cleansed, and the deaf hear, the dead are raised up, and the poor have the gospel preached to them. (Matt. 11:5)

A study of healing in its various manifestations reveals strong support for this indissoluble relationship between salvation and wholeness.

The distinguished philosopher William E. Hocking wrote:

> Salvation means wholeness, deliverance from all that injures or mutilates, or hinders, the growth of, the personality. It means fullness of life, well-being, strength, power, blessedness, wealth, happiness, righteousness, joy, peace. It is the complete penetration of the human by the divine.[13]

Contemporary theologian Norman Pittenger of Cambridge University not only supports the relationship of salvation and wholeness but also points out that wholeness in relation to the various manifestations of human personality is impossible without experiencing salvation in a spiritual sense. In an article in *Expository Times,* he points out that the "very word 'salvation' means 'health.' In the original Greek *soteria,* which we translate as 'salvation,' can also denote a healthy condition. In Latin, *salus,* which we also translate as 'salvation,' has the related meaning of 'health.' In Anglo-Saxon languages the same is true." Professor Pittenger feels that this is significant "for it shows that there is some deep instinct in man which intimately relates his actual health as a human being with a relationship with others and with God."

The Rev. Dr. Alfred W. Price, longtime international leader in the church's ministry of healing, reminds us that Jesus Christ always spoke to man as a whole. He was not careful to distinguish between moral and physical states. The redemption he preached is of the whole person—body, soul, and spirit.

Chaplain Robert B. Reeves, Jr., who has done extensive clinical work in healing institutions, summarizes the relationship between salvation and wholeness as he writes:

> The biblical words for healing and salvation have the same root meaning in both the Hebrew and the Greek. The meaning is ultimately TO BE MADE WHOLE. The distinction we have made between them, under the influence of the neoplatonic dualism, applying healing to the body and salvation to the soul, is utterly alien to the Bible. Man's health is his salvation, and his salvation is his health; for both are signs of his wholeness as a creature.[14]

The Divine Source of All Healing

All healing is of God. Healing power belongs to God. Medicine does not heal; physicians do not heal; psychiatric therapies do not heal; rest does not heal; climate does not heal. God only uses these means and agents of healing. These words of the eminent French doctor, Ambroise Paré, are found over the gateway of the College of Surgeons in

Paris—"I dressed the patient's wounds; God healed him." Over the entrance to the Columbia-Presbyterian Medical Center in New York City are these words—"For from the Most High cometh healing."

British psychologist Ernest White wrote: "We believe that the gift of healing, whether in the realm of medicine or surgery on the physical plane, or of psychotherapy on the mental plane, comes ultimately from God."[15]

James Van Buskirk states:

> All the healer, whoever he may be, can do is to remove the obstacles to the natural healing powers resident in us. This "vis medicatrix natural," healing power of nature, is what cures, whatever may be the technique, whether by drugs, by surgery, by physiotherapy, by psychoanalysis, by suggestion, by hypnosis, by reeducation, by prayer, by laying on of hands, by anointing.[16]

John Harvey Kellogg, physician and surgeon, founder of sanitariums, author of many books on health, founder and editor for over fifty years of *Good Health Magazine,* says: "The physician does not heal us. Treatments do not heal us. It is the divine power working through these agencies that heals us."

Paul Tournier believes that one of the reasons why people come to him to be treated is because he is weak, and they believe he is relying on God rather than his own efforts. He writes: "I know well that there is not much that I have done, but that it is the work of God."[17]

Early in my healing ministry, I found myself under unusual stress in the preparation for a demanding academic assignment and soon developed an aggravating physical affliction. My esteemed doctor treated me effectively both through medicine and counseling, and I was able to fulfill the assignment. As I neared the successful end of the assignment, I wrote to him from the city in which it was taking place, thanking him for what he had done for me and for making it possible for me to fulfill the assignment. Shortly afterwards I received a letter from him in his longhand, in which among other things he thanked God for being used to help in the healing that God had effected.

Because God is the source of all healing, I do not believe that there are any solitary or exclusive methods of healing. Every legitimate healing method is to be used. A member of my church, who postponed an operation for six weeks because she did not want to manifest any lack of faith in God's healing power and, in the meantime, bled herself into a critically weakened condition, said to me after her successful operation, "Because of wrong ideas I almost bled to death, didn't I?"

I counseled with three teen-agers who had broken their glasses intentionally after a revival meeting because of their newfound faith in the healing power of God. In the meantime, they could not see well enough to read their collateral or to take their tests. I shall never forget that day in my office when they asked me: "We have an appointment with an eye doctor this afternoon. Is it a lack of faith if we wear glasses again?" In response, I remarked emphatically, "It will be a lack of common sense if you do not."

A dear friend summed it all up in a letter when she wrote: "As a result of many prayers, a skilled surgeon, and many lovely cards containing beautiful thoughts, my recovery has been most satisfactory." Truly God heals in so many wonderful ways.

Because God uses every legitimate healing method, the healing ministry of the church should emphasize spiritual preparation for healing through physical and psychological methods. One Sunday afternoon, one of the most dedicated laymen in my church attended the regular monthly healing service. When it came time for healing testimonies, he rose and spoke words like these: "Tomorrow morning I enter the hospital for an operation. In recent weeks I have done everything physically and medically that my doctor has told me to do in preparation for the operation. I am here this afternoon for the laying on of hands so I will also do everything spiritually that I need to do in preparation for it."

All healing is divine. God is the source of it all. This is a deepening conviction in my theology of healing.

I must add one further brief word in this regard. I do not believe that devils can heal. I am reminded of what was spoken after Jesus healed a blind man: "How could a demon give sight to blind people?" (John 10:21 TEV). Satan's purpose is to keep persons from wholeness and to rob them of it. Jesus Christ came that men might have life and have it abundantly (v. 10).

This chapter, and the preceding one, have been a presentation of my theology of healing. What I have written makes sense to me in the light of what the Scriptures reveal about the creative relationship of God to his creatures and his redemptive purposes for them and his world. Such a theology supports me as I engage in a healing ministry. Such a theology makes the church for me a healing agency according to the plan of God.

I share the conviction of my esteemed friend, Laurence Blackburn, longtime leader in the healing ministry:

> God wants you to be well. His desire for you is an abundant, joyful life. His will for you is that you be a radiant witness to his love and care. His purpose for you is that your wholeness contribute to the healing of a sick and broken world. . . . God's power within us makes possible the Kingdom of God.[18]

QUESTIONS FOR REFLECTION

1. Why is there a tendency among some religious people (including Christians) to depreciate the human body?

2. How do you relate the will of God to such things as sin, sickness, accident, calamity, death?

3. Did Jesus use the words "saved" and "made whole" interchangeably?

4. Is a person really saved if he or she does not want to be made whole?

5. Can a person be whole who is not saved, in the New Testament sense?

6. Some people sincerely believe that devils can heal. What do you think?

THE HEALING STEPS

We come now to an exceeding practical area in relation to healing. We must have a clear understanding of the personal steps to be taken in seeking healing.

God's universe everywhere gives evidence of plan and design. This is an orderly universe. God's laws are continually in operation. The cosmos is sustained through such divine orderliness. Henry Drummond reminds us that "nothing that happens in this world happens by chance. God is a God of order. Everything is arranged upon definite principles, and never at random. The world, even the religious world, is governed by law."[19]

Spiritual experiences are governed by law. If a person wishes to be saved in a Christian sense, there are certain steps that will be taken. If a child of God wishes to enter into the Spirit-filled life, there are well-defined steps in receiving the fullness of the Holy Spirit. Prayers are answered, divine guidance is received, character is achieved, ministry is fulfilled—all as a result of cooperation with the divine laws that have been revealed in the Holy Scriptures.

E. D. Starbuck, eminent psychologist, declares that "there is no event in the spiritual life which does not occur in accordance with immutable laws." Quoting Henry Drummond again, "The Christian life is not casual but causal. All nature is a standing protest against the absurdity of expecting to secure spiritual effects, or any effects, without the employment of appropriate causes."[20]

Just so, God's healing, through any of the various healing methods, is to be sought along a clearly marked path. The healing process is not magical or irrational. There are definite healing steps to be taken by the person seeking healing.

I recall an experience in a healing mission in Mississippi. Several members of a family interviewed me early in the mission seeking to find out why a member of their family had not yet been healed because he had been prayed for. I remember one of their comments: "We called in the neighbors and prayed, but nothing happened." In response I tried to explain that in an effective healing ministry there must be spiritual preparation for even the praying. We dare not presume that God automatically responds to us whether or not there is proper spiritual content to our religious performances.

It is imperative to keep in mind the laws of healing. I believe these laws are discovered in six healing steps. It cannot be established precisely that these steps must be taken in the order in which they are discussed. In the light of personal circumstances, it could well be that there is a different succession of the steps in some instances. It can be affirmed, however, that sometime in the healing process every one of the steps, and the spiritual stage that each represents, must be experienced.

Relaxation

The first step is that of *relaxation.* "Be still, and know that I am God" (Ps. 46:10 RSV). A literal Hebrew translation of the above verse is "Relax, and discover that I am God." The word "relaxation" means "to be loose again." The opposite of relaxation is tension.

In seeking healing the body must be relaxed and freed of all tension. In fact, the body must be forgotten so that the mind can concentrate on God and on his healing power. Just as the sky cannot be reflected on troubled waters, so the presence of God cannot be realized by a restless body. We cannot truly contact God except in stillness.

The mind must be relaxed. The mind must cease to reason. The person must not think about his or her problems. The mind must center on eternal affirmations, such as the prophetic words "In quietness and in trust shall be your strength" (Isa. 30:15 RSV).

There must also be soul-relaxation. The spirit must open itself to God: "Be still, and know that I am God." Having attained an attitude of stillness, the greatest of all thoughts will then come stealing into one's mind. We then know that "I am God"—that God is the One who is at work, that God is the One who does the healing. A marginal reading of Psalm 62:5 states: "My soul, be thou silent unto God." Such silence springs from the absolute certainty that God knows what he is doing.

The power of God is in response to the stillness of the soul. Bryan Green, the British Anglican evangelist, tells a lovely fable about the ocean. The sea, it is imagined, was one day feeling discontented. Disillusioned, it hated living at its low sea level when above it were drifting some lovely little clouds, scudding along before the wind. The sea grumbled to itself, "I don't see why I should be living down here at this low level. Why can't I live higher up, up where the clouds are?" And so, in its discontent and anger, the sea began to lash itself into fierce high waves, flinging the foam of its spray high up into the air, yet always it fell down again to its low level of living. Then, one day, the sun smiled down on the sea, and said kindly: "You want to live on a higher level? Then don't fret yourself and strain and struggle. Lie still and look up." So the sea lay still, very still, and looked up. A warm wind arose, the sun came down and carried some of the water up into heaven, and presently there were fresh white clouds moving overhead.

Purging

The second step is that of *purging.* "If we walk in the light, as he is in the light, we have fellowship one with another, and the blood of Jesus Christ his Son cleanseth us from all sin" (I John 1:7). The conscious mind and soul must be forgiven of all wrongdoing and wrong relationships. God's healing power can work only in those who are living in accord with his laws.

The subconscious mind must be cleared of all sinful states and negative emotions, so that the healing power of God can flow through it. "Blessed are the pure in heart, for they shall see God" (Matt. 5:8 RSV). A person must rid himself of anything and everything that keeps God from working effectively in his life.

James Denney helps us to understand what it means to "walk in the light": (1) to confess our sins without reserve, never to explain, extenuate, excuse them, (2) to accept our responsibility without reserve for our sins, (3) to refuse to keep a secret hold on our sins in our hearts after we have confessed them to God and received his forgiveness.

Much time can be wasted in praying for people who cannot or will not confess their sins. If the sick one will not be reconciled to just one other person, prayer may be quite ineffectual. If we do not "leave there thy gift and go and be reconciled," prayer will not help. If the sick one has some bitter grief or sense of injustice that he cannot share, God cannot help until it comes out. The sick person may not be committing outward sins but may be experiencing some wrong attitude or unwholesome state of mind or soul that may seem justifiable to him because of the circumstances involved. If a person has been wronged, it is not always possible to punish the wrongdoer, but it is always possible for the injured one to forgive, even though it takes time and effort.

On the evening following the regular monthly healing service in my church, I overheard two ladies talking in the church office. The one who had attended the healing service said to the other who had a definite physical need: "Why weren't you at the healing service yesterday?" The second lady replied immediately: "I have some things to fix up before I can ask God for healing."

I talked one afternoon with a minister and his wife about the husband's critical need of physical healing. Not having talked with them before, I asked them to take a few minutes to review the healing steps together. (I have a specially prepared printed page containing all the healing steps that I use in my ministry of healing.) When the couple came to this step of purging, the husband looked at me and, pointing to his wife, remarked: "If this is true, then she and I have some things to get right between us before I can go on with the other healing steps."

Clarification

The third step is that of *clarification.* "And Jesus stood still, and called them [the blind men] and said, 'What do you want me to do for you?'" (Matt. 20:32 RSV). The response of the blind men was immediate and specific. They did not say: "Anything you want to do for us," or "Help us to have a good feeling," or "Just give us a blessing, Lord." They answered at the point of their deepest physical need: "Let our eyes be opened" (v. 33 RSV).

The person seeking healing must not be vague or general. One must be sure of the area in which healing is needed. Some people are not sick, they are only tired. They need rest. Some people are not sick, they only think they are sick. They need to learn how to discipline their thoughts away from illness in the direction of wholeness.

But many people are actually sick. The exact area of such illness must be identified. Some are sick physically. Some are ill mentally and emotionally. Some are sick spiritually. Some are ill in more than one area at the same time.

When we know the area of our need of healing, then we are to present our request clearly and specifically to the Great Physician. The person seeking healing must be specific, telling God exactly the area in which he or she needs healing. The need must be visualized exactly and the desire vocalized specifically.

Consecration

The fourth step is that of *consecration.* "Whether we live therefore, or die, we are the Lord's" (Rom. 14:8). One of the conditions of divine healing is this spiritual attitude of the absolute relinquishment of one's life to the will of God. There must be complete surrender to God on the part of the person seeking healing. If the will of God be that health is restored immediately, then let God be praised. If health cannot be restored at once, then let the seeker realize that God is in every human circumstance and that ultimately his purpose will be made manifest.

Just so, the seeker after healing must be characterized by a sincere willingness to glorify God and to live for others. Healing, when received, cannot be hoarded selfishly. The renewed strength and the restored health are to be dedicated to God for the blessing and the service of others.

When we really take the step of consecration we do not have to include in our healing prayers the words "if it be thy will." We have settled the matter of God's will. Hopefully we were the Lord's before we were sick. Since taking the step of purging, we are the Lord's even though we are sick. We are the Lord's as we seek healing. We will be the Lord's, whatever the consequences.

Jesus insisted on a positive faith: "What things soever ye desire, when ye pray, believe that ye receive them, and ye shall have them" (Mark 11:24). "If you ask anything in my name, I will do it" (John 14:14 RSV). Hence, when we pray for healing, we must not make any reservation by adding "If it be thy will." Jesus never taught that the will of God was ever against healing. But he did teach that unbelief could stand in the way of healing. Therefore, all if's must be excluded from prayers for healing.

Anticipation

The fifth step, and indeed a strategic step, is that of *anticipation.* This is the step of anticipatory faith. "Faith is the substance of things hoped for, the evidence of things not seen" (Heb. 11:1). As one seeks healing, there must be an eager expectancy, the attitude of an active faith. Never must a seeker think in terms of failure. Always there is the anticipation of God fulfilling what he has already promised.

In writing of faith and its relation to healing, Albert E. Day gives a practical analysis of what is involved in an active faith. Among other things, he reminds us that faith is the acceptance of a thing as beneficial—the employment of prayer to effect healing. Faith is also the reception of an idea as true—the idea that healing power is available. Faith is, likewise, the acceptance of a personality as real—one's own personality as a psychosomatic reality, subject to spiritual laws as well as physical; and God's personality as master of both the physical and spiritual realms.

Thus faith means absolute fidelity to all these ideas: a fidelity that manifests itself in a certain quality of life—living by prayer, living in quest for and in acceptance of the healing, living as if spiritual laws were as important as physical laws, living as if God were Master in both areas and would demonstrate his mastery if one will give him the required cooperation, living in God's life-giving power.

Dr. Day points out that faith for healing is even more; it also involves the use of the imagination. Like every other faculty, the Christian's imagination is to be sanctified. Such a sanctified imagination in relation to healing demands that one should sustain in imagination only pictures of God at work in his body: annihilating germs, subduing toxins, repairing diseased tissues. Lightfoot's translation of Hebrews 11:1 suggests that "faith is that which gives reality to things hoped for." Just as a person must be specific as he visualizes his need for healing, so must he be able to visualize himself as healed in the particular area of need when his prayer is answered.

One of the chief obstacles to healing is the old mind-set—one's preoccupation with disease or some habitual notion about its incurability, or some stubbornness of opinion that, once having denied the possibility of spiritual healing, is reluctant to admit its error. God is equally helpless before intellectual doubt and negative imaginations.

In seeking healing there must always be the spirit of anticipation. Kathryn Kuhlman, who carried on an internationally known ministry of healing, employed a startling spiritual technique in which she appointed a certain day for the healing of the person for whom she was praying. On that day she would believe that the person was being healed, and she asked the person being prayed for to believe for a miracle on that day.

One is reminded of what we read in the Gospels about certain of the healings performed by Jesus. On more than one occasion the person was healed in the same hour that belief was exercised. "His servant was healed in the selfsame hour" (Matt. 8:13). "Her daughter was made whole from that very hour" (15:28). "Yesterday at the seventh hour the fever left him. So the father knew that it was at the same hour, in the which Jesus said unto him, Thy son liveth" (John 4:52-53).

In commenting on the above technique of Kathryn Kuhlman, Canon Jim Glennon, who carries on a ministry of healing in St. Andrew's Cathedral, Sydney, Australia, testifies:

> I have come to the place of being able to act on the insights and practice of Miss Kuhlman. I have begun to set aside a day for the person's healing for whom I am praying. I believe on that day God will raise him/her up. I observe the whole day with that thought in mind, so that it is a day of believing, a day of accepting, a day of decision, a day of praise—that on *this* day God is healing this person, or persons. I pray to the point where I have no reservation and leave open no "back doors" for me to find some way out.[21]

I have learned in my healing ministries that this matter of anticipatory faith is crucial. I have not known of a case where this kind of faith was present, without any doubts whatever, when healing did not result. Far too often a person confesses that he or she thought there was genuine faith, but actually there were damaging inward doubts.

I conducted a healing service for a seminary couple who were seeking the healing needed in order that they might have a child. Medical science had already confirmed that it was not an impossibility. As I discussed with them this step of anticipatory faith, I asked: "Can you now hear your own baby crying?"

Later in the book I share with you the stories of the healings of George Nakajima, then a Seminary student, and of Dorothy Davis, then a missionary in Zaire. When you read their stories, look for the step of anticipatory faith. George said, "I immediately imagined myself healed by God and back in Japan witnessing to my own people." Dorothy wrote in her Bible after the healing service: "On May 2, 1966, in the prayer room of Estes Chapel, Asbury Seminary, God healed my body."

Much more recently I talked with a businessman about his healing experience after a serious heart attack. He told me that one afternoon in the hospital, while he was thinking and praying about healing, he looked out the hospital window upon the busy city street below. Suddenly he was able to visualize himself among the busy throng walking the same street. He said that from that moment he had an inward sense that he would be healed. This was anticipatory faith, inspired by God's Spirit.

When these five healing steps have been taken—relaxation, purging, clarification, consecration, anticipatory faith—there has been created what Emily Gardiner Neal describes as "the proper climate for healing." Like all the rest of God's creative processes, the proper climate is necessary for new life and the manifestations of all the "quickening powers of God's Spirit."

On a Sunday evening within recent months my wife and I were invited to participate in healing conversation and prayer with a couple, the wife having just returned from the hospital after surgery for cancer. I do not remember a time in my healing ministry when a more suitable climate had already been created for healing. The wife greeted us at the door, her usual cheerful, gracious self, and told us almost immediately that she had attended church that morning. Every succeeding moment of that evening together was in an atmosphere of positive attitudes and radiant faith. The person never seemed to tire at all. Continually there was an expression of gratitude for loved ones and friends.

She testified to no panic, no perplexity as to why this had happened to her, and no pain. She spoke of her perfect peace, her complete confidence in God, and her assurance that God was healing her. She said that during the hours and days of her healing she was determined to surround herself only with persons who are positive in outlook and confident in prayer.

When it came time for healing prayer she asked for such a time of prayer to be in a totally relaxed atmosphere devoid of any artificial prayer techniques. She just wanted all of us in our love for God and one another to reach out to God simply and in faith for his perfect healing power. After I said the amen to the healing prayer, she commented confidently, "I know that God is healing me."

Appropriation

The final and climactic healing step is that of *appropriation.* "I can do all things through Christ which strengtheneth me" (Phil. 4:13). The seeker accepts what God has promised, begins acting in the strength of the healing power received, and is grateful to God for the reality of the healing power in one's life. "Father, I thank thee," is the consummation of the personal appropriation of the divine blessings.

Of great importance in the appropriation of God's healing power is the influence of a person's previously made decision of what his or her response will be to such healing. Laurence Blackburn suggests the following responses when one is healed: (a) do not look behind, but look ahead to a life of new and greater dimension, (b) give your witness of what God has done for you, (c) let your words of witness be followed by deeds of dedication, (d) let your gift of health be dedicated to the church, (e) be willing to be a channel of healing to others, (f) always be humble, (g) always be thankful.[22]

QUESTIONS FOR REFLECTION

1. Does the emphasis upon spiritual laws in this chapter confuse you in any way in relation to a gospel of grace?

2. How can a person learn to relax in the scriptural sense of relaxation?

3. How can you identify "the light of Christ" when it shines upon you? How does one distinguish the light from mere personal prejudices or compulsions or from the opinions of others?

4. How can a person discover accurately the area or areas of his or her need of healing?

5. Distinguish between the kinds of prayers that must include the words "if it be thy will" and those that do not require such a condition.

6. What are the factors that encourage anticipatory faith? What are the hindrances to anticipatory faith?

HOW TO BE HEALED

E. Stanley Jones has reminded us of seven ways by which God heals:

1. God heals through surgeons. Medical history is replete with cases where individuals have been healed as the result of an operation.

2. God heals through physicians. God has laid up in nature various remedies that medical science is in the process of discovering. Such remedies are to be used wisely, but never overused or abused.

3. God can heal through mental suggestion. A person can suggest sickness to himself, and he will become sick. On the other hand, you can think health, and talk health to yourself, and it aids the healing process. How often healing through physical and psychological methods has been aided by constructive mental, emotional, and spiritual attitudes within the patient.

4. God can heal through climate. Although this can be overstressed—for the real climate of health or ill health is within a person—nevertheless, some natural climates are more conducive to health and some are more conducive to disease.

5. God heals through a person's deliverance from underlying fears, loneliness, self-centeredness, purpose-lessness, resentments, guilts, that produce disease.

6. God heals through the direct operation of the Spirit of God upon the body. The apostle Paul writes in Romans 8:11: "But if the Spirit of him that raised up Jesus from the dead dwell in you, he that raised up Christ from the dead shall also quicken your mortal bodies by his Spirit that dwelleth in you." There is no nerve or tissue that is beyond the healing touch of the Spirit of God.

7. God also heals through the final cure—the resurrection of the body. Some illnesses must await the final cure of

the resurrection. This does not mean that God will not heal. Rather, it means that he has postponed healing for some, to await the final cure of eternity. He will heal later on. In the meantime he gives the sufferer power not merely to bear his suffering, but to use it, until the final release.[23]

The first healing article I penned after my father's passing in 1969 was entitled "The Healing of Eternity." We had prayed sincerely for his physical healing. Nevertheless, God chose for him healing through the final cure.

Prayer groups around the world prayed for months for the healing of my sister-in-law, a dedicated missionary in Kŏrea. She was in the midst of a magnificently effective missionary career, and there seemed so much for her to continue doing. One Saturday afternoon, as my wife sat alone meditating, she heard the voice of her sister saying: "Mardie, I'm healed." Immediately my wife began thanking the Lord for what had happened. Within a matter of minutes the telephone rang. It was an overseas call from a friend in Korea informing us of her passing. "Mardie, I'm healed"—true—but it was the healing of eternity.

Against this background of the various ways in which God heals, and keeping in mind that six of the seven ways relate to us in our mortal existence, let us consider the question, How can a person be healed? The following guidelines should prove helpful:

1. Discover whether you are really sick or whether you only think you are sick. Some persons are not actually sick—they only think they are. A doctor said of such a person: "For forty years Tom has suffered agonies from imaginitis, scarcoma, apprehenditis, and general fearosis of living."

Professional diagnosis is needed to establish the actuality of one's illness in any area. Medical science establishes the reality of physical and mental/emotional illness. Spiritual counselors, adequately trained and practically oriented, are able to diagnose sickness of the inner spirit. If a person is not actually sick but continues to believe that he or she is sick, then the healing needed is the discipline of his thoughts away from illness and in the direction of health, vitality, and adequate strength in Jesus Christ.

2. A person may need to discover whether he or she is really sick or only tired. Fatigue is usually a symptom of sickness, but not all fatigue is caused by physical illness. If it is discovered that a person is physically or mentally exhausted, then the cure is rest. Some of the healing movements have prescribed rest treatments. A body will recuperate from mere physical tiredness in twenty-four to forty-eight hours.

But there are also psychological and spiritual factors that cause fatigue: inner guilt, oversensitivity, self-centeredness, boredom, fear, worry, indecision, inferiorities, resentments. Such psychological and spiritual factors must be faced honestly. The needed rest comes only when the basic causes are dealt with decisively.

3. When it is established by medical science or professional spiritual counseling that a person is actually sick, then the first imperative is to clarify the particular area of illness and to discover the proper procedure for seeking healing for the particular need.

Sickness can affect any part of the human personality: body, mind-emotions, soul. If the body is sick, physical health must be restored. If the mind or emotions are sick, mental health must be achieved. If the soul is basically sick, out of harmony with God, and in wrong relation to life and to others, then forgiveness must be sought and a life of holiness begun.

I recall two women who together counseled with me previous to a healing service during a healing mission. The first asked me: "Can I be healed from a dependence upon cigarettes during periods of stress and strain?" Her friend within a matter of minutes asked: "And can I be healed of lustful desires that have led me into an adulterous life?"

I can never forget the words of a woman kneeling at an altar for healing prayer when she looked up into my face and asked:

"Can I be healed of the agony I have been living in since I consented to an abortion?"

4. Suppose the illness is basically physical, then the type of bodily sickness must be identified. There are two types of bodily sickness: functional and organic, or structural. A functional illness is one in which even though there is nothing wrong with an organ or a part of the structure of the body, it is malfunctioning because of wrong attitudes or emotions within the person. Doctors estimate that four out of five illnesses are functional. On the other hand, an organic or structural illness is the evidence that something is wrong with an organ or a part of the structure of the body.

5. If the bodily illness is discovered to be of the functional type, then healing is to be sought along two lines in accordance with the diagnosis of both cause and manifestation.

a. If the sickness is functional in both manifestation and cause, then it must be dealt with mentally, emotionally, and spiritually. Such destructive emotions as guilt, self-centeredness, fear, anxiety, worry, resentments, hatred, ill will, and inferiorities, which cause functional illness, must be brought to the level of the conscious mind, confessed, and replaced by their opposite positive emotions. Such a replacement is made possible by the Spirit of Jesus Christ operating upon the normal functions of the human personality.

b. If the illness has distinctly organic or structural manifestations but has been caused by functional disturbances, physical methods should be employed to remedy the organic or structural maladies that are present. Then psychological/spiritual methods must be used to remove the basic psychosomatic causes of such organic or structural manifestations. Psychiatrists who operate within a Christian frame of reference should be permitted to give their diagnosis and prescribe their remedies.

6. If the illness is distinctly organic or structural in both manifestations and cause, all reasonable, normal, physical

methods should be employed. Reputable physicians and surgeons should be consulted, and their mature advice followed. Proved medical methods and treatments should be utilized.

7. If the illness is definitely mental or emotional, careful steps must be taken to receive all the necessary healing aids. There are many causes of mental/emotional illness. Sometimes it is hereditary and thus congenital. Sometimes it is the result of psychological disturbances and maladjustments within the chemistry of the body. Recent years have witnessed great strides in psychiatry in relation to chemical imbalances within the physical body and the resulting ill effects upon mind and emotions.

At other times emotional illness is the result of personal tensions and pressures and consequent depletion of nerve energy within the person. For an enlightening study of this particular phase of emotional illness, I recommend a booklet by Alfred W. Price, International Warden of the Order of St. Luke the Physician, entitled *The Healing of Nervous Disorders by Spiritual Therapy.*

I am convinced that whenever there is clearly indicated mental/emotional illness, a trained professional should be consulted by the patient. In such cases scientific help is imperative. How fortunate for a patient when a professional psychologist or psychiatrist with a distinctly Christian orientation can be consulted.

But let it be kept in mind that mere psychological analysis is not adequate for the healing of mental/emotional illness. Such analysis may help a person to understand both the nature and cause of his illness but in itself cannot provide full healing. To use a term that has been popularized by Dr. Price, the sick person needs psychosynthesis as well as psychoanalysis. People are made well in their minds and emotions and nerves only as Jesus Christ speaks peace in the depths of their personalities and as God's Spirit aids them to live a life disciplined in the direction of wholeness.

8. By whatever method healing is being sought, prayer is to

be employed as a constant spiritual aid. The person seeking healing must be in a continual attitude of prayer and, if capable, should participate in personal acts of prayer. Certainly intercessory prayer groups (these will be discussed in a later chapter) should be active on behalf of a person seeking healing through physical or psychological methods. Prayer makes the person receptive to healing power; prayer provides guidance for those who are healing agents; prayer releases the healing power of the Great Physician into particular situations.

9. But what if reasonable and normal physical or psychological methods, even when used prayerfully, prove to be ineffective and the person is not healed? I believe that it is at this point that there is the opportunity for a person to seek healing through the direct divine activity. In chapter 4 we discussed such healing through the direct divine activity as one of the relationships between the Christian faith and healing. The seeking of such healing calls for a definite healing ministry on behalf of a person. Care is exercised in leading a person through the healing steps to the climactic moments of the laying on of hands or anointing with oil.

In the seeking of healing in any area of the human personality the healing steps are of supreme importance. As we take these healing steps, we focus our total selves upon the healing presence of God. We remind ourselves that God is present, and that his presence is a loving presence, a healing presence. In the stillness of God's presence we enter more deeply into the realization of his love and power. Because God loves us we know that we can entrust ourselves—body, mind, emotions, soul, will—to the healing power of his presence.

Into God's hands, therefore, we surrender the keys of our total being, that he may unlock every door and by his Spirit enter into every area of our need and possess us with his healing presence. The healing presence within brings love, joy, peace, power.

10. It is very possible that in the diagnosis of one's sickness the basic causes will be found in the spiritual areas of one's life rather than primarily in one's body or mind. I recall an article written by Leslie Weatherhead that was entitled "Her Conversion Was Her Cure." Much illness is the direct consequence of wrong relationships—to God and to other persons. Such estrangement is caused by self-centered rebellion, putting one's self in the place of God, hence the refusal to yield one's self to the authority of God and to the lordship of Jesus Christ.

The cure for spiritual sickness is confession of sin and a total submission of one's self to God, who has revealed himself in and through Jesus Christ.

The person seeking to be made spiritually whole must affirm reverently, as a life-and-death matter, the following in the presence of God:

a. I need to be made whole at the very depths of my being.

b. I confess my sins, particularly my sin of self-centeredness.

c. I accept Jesus Christ as my Savior from sin and as the One who is able to make me whole within.

d. I submit to the lordship of Jesus Christ in my daily life.

e. I will gladly witness to others concerning the new life of wholeness that Jesus Christ has effected within me.

QUESTIONS FOR REFLECTION

1. How do you react to the idea that some persons are not really sick: they only think they are sick, *or* they are only tired?
2. Can tiredness ever be considered a sin?
3. Can you accept every legitimate healing method as divine healing?
4. Is there a difference in the exercise of faith in relation to healing primarily through physical and psychological means and healing primarily through spiritual methods?
5. Should we expect to be healed from organic and structural illness as well as from psychosomatic sickness?
6. How do you know when you have received God's healing power?

PERSONS WHO HAVE BEEN HEALED

It seems practical to follow the preceding chapter on "How to Be Healed" with the story of some persons who have been healed. Healing literature is replete with the record of personal healings. Every book listed in the Bibliography that appears at the close of these chapters offers deeply moving testimonies to the healing power of God. In these pages I am intending, however, to limit the witnesses to healing to those persons whom I know, several of whom have experienced healing in ministries with which I have been personally related.

I participated in a Bible conference with a man who had been marvelously restored to ministry as a result of healing through heart surgery. He testified that he went to sleep under anesthesia with the psalmist's words in his mind: "I shall awake with thy likeness."

At the same conference was a gifted violinist. Some months before he had been severely burned on his hand when he automatically reached to grab a piece of hot metal as it was slipping from a tray. Among the remarks of the attending physician in the emergency room was the statement that he would probably never be able to play his violin again. But the healing miracle took place—within eight days he was playing again and as beautifully as ever.

During the course of the conference, a young man was healed of a serious allergy reaction on his face. He testified afterwards that as he took the step of faith, he claimed the Scripture promise: "He is the health of my countenance."

After a healing ministry during a traditional camp meeting, I received a revealing letter from one who had been in attendance. Here are pertinent parts of that letter which give witness to a spiritual healing:

> I want to thank you for having a healing service. I really did come with anticipation for physical healing. Before your

preaching, I did not realize there were wrong motives for it. Today, God has opened my understanding so much, that I have had a spiritual healing. That's the one thing I did not think I needed. If anyone had told me that I had resentment in my heart toward God himself, I would not have believed it. I wondered why it was hard for me to pray, and I have missed the joy that I once knew in my heart. My eyes are on Jesus now, and I know how much He suffered for us.

I pray that God can use me to help bring the healing ministry back into our church.

During the course of a professional assignment, a guest clergyman who serves on the staff of one of the most active churches spiritually in America, revealed in personal conversation the existence of a serious eye problem which so restricted his vision that he could no longer drive his automobile after dark. Interested friends participated in a healing service for him, and immediately there was improvement in his vision. He testified to this on the following morning. After his return to the church, he wrote: "My vision has continued much strengthened, more than I have experienced in months. . . . I have been driving unattended after dark with marvelous freedom. . . . I am seeing many things with a great deal more clarity."

A friend told me of his being healed of what he called "psychosomatic cold-catching." He said that previously every kind of stress resulted in a cold. But he surrendered his total self to the healing Christ. He now testifies: "Since I have been in Christ I don't need to be sick. Whenever I feel myself getting sick, I realize that it is in relation to some spiritual problem that needs to be solved."

A wife told me recently of a marvelous healing in marital relationships. There was really no trouble, as such, between the husband and wife. But a previously experienced circumstance with psychological implications had continued to be a barrier to a completely satisfying relationship. Through healing prayer the afflicted husband was delivered, and a real honeymoon began after twenty-two years of married life.

For several years I have taught an elective course entitled "Healing and the Christian Faith." Every year there are testimonies to personal healings as a result of the course. One student shared with me his experience of healing in every area of his life. Because of the need to provide financial support for his family while he was in school, he became physically exhausted as he tried to fulfill two outside jobs. This exhaustion led to mental anguish and despair about being able to finish seminary. There were even spiritual overtones—he was beginning to undertrust God to help him handle the whole affair. But he experienced healing. Here are his own words:

> When I came to the end of myself, I asked God to heal these three areas of my life. I received the laying on of hands, and the prayer of the intercessor was amazingly accurate to my situation. God met me there. He had been available *all* the time. I just hadn't acknowledged him.
>
> I was healed. Not that instant! I was given new courage and direction. God healed me from the top down—SPIRITUALLY—EMOTIONALLY—and then PHYSICALLY. To him be the glory!

Another young man who was being victimized by the devastations of guilt and fear because of past unfortunate experiences in his life finally came to the place where he could believe that God willed wholeness for even him. He asked the Holy Spirit to heal him of any guilt of the past and to deliver him from any fear of the future. The healing miracle took place. He stopped needing medication for his nerves, and a new dimension of healing was added to his life. Each day became a new opportunity to experience the continual healing power of the Spirit.

Another person was healed of an emotional disturbance that had physical symptoms that had cursed him daily for eighteen years.

One of the most thrilling physical healings with which I have been related was that experienced by George Nakajima, now a pastor in Osaka, Japan, and a teacher in Osaka Christian College. In response to my request, he wrote the story of his healing, and it was published under the title "The Third Prayer."

One Sunday night after returning home from conducting a meeting in the church of a friend in Ohio, I discovered that I was bleeding inwardly. By the time I was admitted to the Good Samaritan Hospital in Lexington, Kentucky, I had lost two-thirds of my blood and was terribly weak.

I spent nine weeks in the hospital and had three major operations upon my stomach and intestines. Those operations took from three to four hours. Even though I had had three operations on my intestines before coming to this country, this recent hospital experience was to have the most meaning for me, both physically and spiritually, for I have been healed and have returned to my studies.

My healing is due to the prayers of many friends, both known and unknown. Of course, God used brilliant doctors, excellent hospital equipment and highly-developed medical science. But there are many things about my healing that cannot be explained even by the doctors. My doctor told one of my friends that my case was a miracle.

One week after the first operation in the Lexington hospital, my small intestine became blocked and I had severe pain. The doctors then performed the second operation on me, working four hours. But even after the operation, things did not go well. Food would not pass through me. So, ten days after the second operation I had a third operation. Even after this I was kept on the critical list because I was not eating and was extremely weak. I could not even digest liquids.

Those weeks in the hospital were significant to me spiritually. Physically I suffered much. But I also gained spiritual victories. Each one of the operations confronted me with a spiritual crisis. At the time of the first operation, I prayed for God's help because I worried about my family, my school program, my finances, etc. But I was so selfish in my praying.

86

At the time of the second operation, I prayed because I was afraid. I was afraid of the suffering, because I had suffered so much after the first operation. Ironically, the second operation was the hardest of the three.

I remember the day before the third operation. I prayed sincerely: "Lord, forgive me. I was wrong. I was so selfish. I do not know whether I can make it this time because I am so weak. But I know one thing, I need peace. Give me Thy peace, and Thy will be done." I remember that immediately wonderful peace came into my heart. Fear and worry were gone, and my heart was so calm. I praised and thanked God.

The third operation took more than four hours. But as I awakened in the recovery room I had peace and not as much pain as before. This victory of faith was a wonderful experience.

A week later, pain came back. My doctor came to me and said, "George, maybe we will have to operate again. If so, it may take all day." I prayed again, "Thy will be done."

It was at this time that the idea of a special healing service was suggested to me by my pastor, the Rev. Clyde Van Valin. He helped to prepare me for the healing service.

Within a short time three men of God—my pastor; Mr. John Fitch, a dedicated layman; and the President of the Seminary—came to my hospital room for the healing service. They anointed me, laid hands on me, and prayed for my healing.

During the healing service, the President of the Seminary reminded me of the healing steps. I was really impressed by his statement that faith must have some imagination in it. He said, "Imagine yourself healed by God and for the glory of God." I immediately imagined myself healed by God and back in Japan witnessing to my own people.

I want to testify that from the time of the healing service in my hospital room I began to recover. I amazed the doctors. There was no fourth operation. My meals were increased little by little. My body began to function more normally.

I returned to my home. Now I am back in the Seminary. I have been healed by the mercy and power of God.[24]

The story of Dorothy Davis, longtime missionary in Zaire, revives deeply meaningful memories. I recall the morning when I participated in a healing service for her.

In 1966 a biopsy performed on her body in the mission hospital aroused fear as to a possible malignancy. A second biopsy was performed, and the specimen sent to the United States for a more definite word. When the word came via cable from the doctor in New York, it was diagnosed as lymphal sarcoma, and she was instructed to return to the States immediately for radiation treatments.

Shortly after her arrival, the healing service was held for her. I recall the occasion as a time when the healing presence of God was unusually manifest. Mrs. Davis testified that during the service she took the six healing steps and she was assured that what God had promised he was able to perform. When she returned to her mother's home, she wrote at once on the flyleaf of her Bible: "On May 2, 1966, in the prayer room of Estes Chapel, Asbury Seminary, God healed my body."

Let the rest of the story be told in her own words:

Two days after the healing service, Joe and I flew from Kentucky to Bethesda, Maryland, where the doctor from our mission board in New York had arranged for me to enter the hospital for radiation treatments. This hospital is part of the National Institutes of Health, and doctors and pathologists there do extensive research in the particular type of malignancy that I had. We had brought the slides from the second biopsy performed in the Congo back to the States with us and after the pathologists reviewed both sets of slides (from the two biopsies) they gave us this report: The first biopsy definitely showed a low-grade malignancy—lymphal sarcoma—but the nodes removed from the second biopsy, although showing "peculiar" looking cells, could not be definitely determined as malignant; and since there had been much discussion and controversy, the doctors wanted to perform a third biopsy to be absolutely sure before starting extensive radiation.

So on the following Monday, the surgeon removed more lymph nodes and told us that the report would be ready on Wednesday. On Wednesday afternoon the doctor talked with

Joe and me. Although the pathologists would not have the report until the next day, he was so sure that the diagnosis would be the same as the first biopsy that he wanted me to have two months of radiation treatments followed by annual checkups. After the doctor told me this, I shared with him my experience and told him I knew I had been healed two days before coming to Bethesda and firmly believed that everything was all right.

The next day, Thursday afternoon, the doctor came again to tell us that that morning six of the nation's top pathologists had reviewed and discussed for several hours the nodes removed from the third biopsy, and although they said they were "peculiar" looking, they could not definitely be diagnosed as malignant! As a result no radiation treatments were needed. I was dismissed from the hospital on the following Monday, with a checkup slated for the latter part of August.

In concluding his talk with Joe and me on that Thursday afternoon, the doctor said, "In some instances we have seen tumors dissolve, and there is no explanation other than by the grace of God."[25]

E. Stanley Jones was a leader in the church's ministry of healing. He experienced personally that the kingdom of God is realism. On the occasion of his passing in 1973 I turned again to his spiritual autobiography, *A Song of Ascents.* In the book he refers to his own miraculous healing in Lucknow in the early years of his ministry in India. Here are his own words:

Almost on arrival in India I had to go to the mountains to recuperate. Back from furlough of a year, the first thing I had to think about was my own health. I came down from the mountains and had to go back again. When I came down the second time, I knew the game was up—I would have to leave the mission field and my work and try to regain my shattered health. It was gone. In that dark hour I was in the Central Methodist Church in Lucknow. The Rev. Tamil David was in charge of the evangelistic services. I was at the back of the church kneeling in prayer, not for myself but for others, when God said to me: "Are you yourself ready for the work to which I have called you?" My reply: "No, Lord, I'm done for. I've reached the end of my resources and I can't go on." "If you'll turn that problem over to me and not worry about it, I'll take care of it." My eager reply: "Lord, I close the bargain right here." I arose from my knees knowing I was a well man. I walked home with a group of missionaries along Cantonment Road. They knew nothing of what was happening within me. But I scarcely touched the earth as I walked along. I was possessed with life and health and peace. For days after that I wondered why I should ever go to bed when bedtime came. I scarcely knew I had a body. I wondered if I should tell this. If I did, it was sink or swim before everybody. But I never hesitated, for I knew this was reality. So I announced it before a large audience in Lucknow. Years later a marble tablet was put up in the wall of this church with this inscription: "Near this spot Stanley Jones knelt a physically broken man and arose a physically well man." This tablet says "physically broken" and "physically well," but this was more than a physical touch. It involved the total person. I was made well and whole—body, mind, and spirit. I was flooded with a sense of energy, of peace, of power, of adequacy.[26]

At the close of his chapter "I Sing of Health," Dr. Jones tells of a moving conversation he had with his own body after a very satisfying physical examination:

I seemed to hear the clapping of hands and the words: "Come on, let's go." My reply: "Dear old body, you've been saying that for the last sixty years and more. We've walked the dusty roads together, we've flown across continents together, you've been uncomplaining even when I've put impossible loads upon you. Thank you for your faithful service, and now you say you'll be faithful until death us do part. When that parting comes, I'll look back at you and salute you and thank you, and I'll say to you: 'When I get my immortal body, I hope there will be a lot of you there incorporated. Thank you again—for everything.'"[27]

I have often been reminded of some remarks that Brother Stanley made about his post-retirement years. Even though he was retired officially at age seventy, he said that he passed retirement age without even so much as a bump. It was then that God promised him at least ten more years. When he reached eighty, God promised him that the next ten years would be the best of his life. After telling this to a group one day, someone asked "How do you know that you are going to live until age ninety?" Brother Stanley replied immediately, "Who said anything about living here on this earth? God merely said that the next ten years of my life would be the best."

How magnificently God fulfilled his promise of wholeness and health to Stanley Jones. At age eighty-nine he entered into the Life Eternal.

QUESTIONS FOR REFLECTION

1. Analyze several of the healing testimonies in this chapter in relation to—
    a. the person's knowledge of specific need of healing;
    b. various healing methods tried;
    c. how the person turned to the Great Physician;
    d. the place of faith in the healing;
    e. how the healing was received;
    f. the evidences of the healing.
2. If you have experienced a healing, write the story of your healing. What factors in your healing are common to those evident in the healings related in this chapter?

HOW TO PRAY FOR HEALING

I want to begin this chapter on an extremely personal note. As far as I can remember, the first article that I ever wrote on healing was in relation to prayer and healing. It was written in 1946, five years before I began my active healing ministry. It appeared in the daily devotional, *The Upper Room,* under the date of August 16.

Writing on the passages in Acts 9:40-41, I penned the following:

> Jesus Christ, the Great Physician, associated prayer and healing in an indissoluble relationship. He prayed before He healed; He thanked God for the healing which He accomplished. He told His disciples that works of healing came only as the result of prayer and fasting.
>
> Moreover, prayer and healing were maintained in a vital association in the Early Christian Church. The first-century Christians were told to resort to prayer, and they were assured that "the prayer of faith shall save the sick, and the Lord shall raise him up."
>
> Just so today, prayers may be utilized as an essential element in all healing. This does not mean to neglect the advantages of modern medicine; rather it emphasizes the power of prayer upon the total personality. Dr. William Sadler, eminent physician, has declared that in neglecting prayer for healing we are neglecting the greatest single power in the healing of disease.

Prayers for Healing Are a Legitimate Spiritual Activity

Many within the fields of religion and medical science have spoken concerning the strategic relationship between prayer and healing. In *Give God a Chance,* W. E. Sangster affirmed that a life open to God in faithful prayer is open to agencies of healing beyond the range of medicine and surgery. Bernard Martin, another clergyman, believes that prayer for the healing of the sick is as justified and essential on the part of the church as the remarkable and continuous efforts of the medical, physical, and mental sciences. It is justified as much as prayer for the cleansing of sinners. Garfield G. Duncan, M.D., has observed that "the wise physician never discounts the healing power of faith, the handmaiden of prayer."

E. Stanley Jones reminds us that prayer can bring a continuous healing:

> If we are identified with Jesus in prayer as cooperation, then His very life comes out in our bodies, quickening them, reconstructing them, making weak tissues and nerves into strong tissues and nerves. . . . This is healing by His very presence within—His life coming out in our mortal bodies. . . . We cultivate His presence, and He in turn permeates us with His health.[28]

Alexis Carrel, M.D., is often quoted in relation to the healing power of prayer:

> Prayer is a force as real as terrestrial gravity. As a physician, I have seen men, after all other therapy had failed, lifted out of disease and melancholy by the serene effort of prayer. It is the only power in the world that seems to overcome the so-called "laws of nature"; the occasions on which prayer has dramatically done this have been termed "miracles."[29]

Prayer is related so efficaciously to healing that it is instinctive for persons of faith to seek healing through prayer. Recently after the family of a friend of ours had received the news that a malignancy had spread through her body, her daughter went at once into the hospital room and said confidently, "Mother, God is greater than cancer."

Healing Prayer in the Bible

The Holy Scriptures recognize this vital relationship between prayer and healing. Prayers for healing are prominent in the Old Testament. Here are a few illustrations: "Heal her now, O God, I beseech thee" (Num. 12:13); "O Lord, heal me" (Ps. 6:2); "Heal me, O Lord, and I shall be healed" (Jer. 17:14).

One recalls the Old Testament narrative of the people being bitten by fiery serpents in the wilderness (Num. 21:6-9). We are told that "the people came to Moses, and said, 'Pray unto the Lord, that he take away the serpents from us.' And Moses prayed for the people." The prayer was heard, for God provided a brazen serpent, which became a symbolical medium of healing to the people. In another era King Hezekiah prayed to God for healing, and his life span was extended fifteen years (II Kings 20).

The New Testament is replete with prayers for healing. During the ministry of Jesus many prayers for healing were addressed to him (see John 4:46-54; Matt. 8:1-13; 9:2-8). Likewise Jesus uttered prayers upon the occasions of his healings (see Matt. 15:29-31; John 11:41-43).

In addition to his actual utterances of prayers for healing, Jesus' teachings contain many specific instructions concerning prayers for healing. For illustration, the one who prays must keep in mind that Jesus wills to heal people (Matt. 8:2-4). Moreover, Jesus is as able to heal as he is to forgive (9:2-8). Likewise, Jesus teaches that faith is essential in healing (8:1, 5-13). Furthermore, it is through the divine power that Jesus effects healing (12:22-37; 9:20-22).

Healing Prayer in the Church

When we study the ministry of the early Christian church, we discover this same prominence of prayers for healing. A detailed study of this subject in the Acts of the Apostles would be rewarding for the interested person (see Acts 3:5; 4:29-30; 5:15-16; 9:11-12, 17-18; 9:32-34, 40-41; 28:3-6).

The ministry of healing and the relationship of prayer to it, as understood in the early church, is summarized in these exhortatory words of the apostle James:

Is any among you afflicted? let him pray. Is any merry? let him sing psalms. Is any sick among you? let him call for the elders of the church; and let them pray over him, anointing him with oil in the name of the Lord: And the prayer of faith shall save the sick, and the Lord shall raise him up; and if he have committed sins, they shall be forgiven him. (James 5:13-15)

During the two centuries after the closing of the New Testament Canon, prayers for healing continued to figure prominently in the ministry of the Christian church. Evelyn Frost, author of the studious volume entitled *Christian Healing,* presents evidence of a valid healing ministry in the early church, as documented in the writings of the ante-Nicene fathers, beginning with Clement of Rome (95 A.D.) and continuing to Lactantius (315 A.D.).

Just so, studies reveal that in every period of church history the practice of Christian praying has included prayers for healing. Today, in the healing ministry of the church, prayer occupies a significantly vital part. In fact, the climax of every healing service is reached in the prayers for healing.

Characteristics of Effective Healing Prayer

The healing power of God flows in response to prayer. At the heart of prayer is sincere spiritual desire. A study of healings reveals the presence of such wholehearted spiritual desire in the supplication that sought such healings. Sometimes the prayer for healing comes from the sufferer himself. Sometimes it came from others who were deeply concerned. At other times the prayer was uttered by the Great Physician himself. But always prayer—total dominant desire—preceded the healing power that resulted.

Healing prayer is to be used in every instance when a person is seeking healing. Healing prayer is not restricted to the use of certain specific healing methods. Since all healing is of God, he can use every legitimate healing agent and method. Prayer should be employed to seek God's active healing presence in the particular situation and circumstance as one is seeking healing. In addition to the divine blessings upon the healing methods being employed, prayer brings the added plus of the possibility of God's direct healing touch.

What, then, are the characteristics of effective healing prayer?

1. Prayer for healing must be *sincere*. It must grow out of a life of prayer. It must arise out of a sense of real need. It must sincerely acknowledge the only valid source of supply—a divine source. There must be a sense of dedication in the use of the results of the healing prayer.

2. Prayer for healing must be *positive*. We must pray affirmatively. Healing prayer must be God-oriented and not patient-centered. The validity of prayer is found in him to whom we pray, rather than in those for whom we pray or in what we pray for.

We must not focus on a person's symptoms of illness when we pray for his or her healing. There are two prominent dangers in focusing upon symptoms. If we are praying in the presence of the ill person, the mere mention of symptoms tends to make even more fixed one's mental pattern of being afflicted. This kind of deepening fixation is a hindrance to anticipatory faith within oneself.

Moreover, there are some intercessors who have certain neurotic tendencies of their own—at least sensitive imaginations. To focus on others' symptoms in prayer may tend to reproduce similar symptoms within such persons. If this should happen, the prayer of faith becomes very difficult.

3. Prayer for healing must be *specific*. A person must be specific, not general, in the request for healing. An individual must visualize exactly his or her need and desire. A person must not be vague. Rather, he or she must tell God exactly what is needed. Being specific in this manner certainly should not be considered presumptuous by a truly dedicated Christian.

4. Prayer for healing must be *anticipatory*. Such prayers must be characterized by an eager expectancy, the attitude of

an active faith. Never must the one who prays think in terms of failure. Always there should be the anticipation of God fulfilling what He has promised.

In our imagination it may help to envisage our Lord standing near the person for whom we are praying and touching the person with his hands. Leslie D. Weatherhead advised: "Do not pray that he/she may get better, because that is putting the cure in the future. Believe that at this very moment Christ is touching that person's body, and that his healing power is being made manifest in that body now."

5. Prayer for healing must be *grateful*. Our final vision of the sufferer must be to see him or her whole and free from illness. In the prayer of faith we must cling to this vision because it is the vision of God willing wholeness. Thus healing prayer always includes an act of thanksgiving, praising God for his will being done in the person for whose healing we are praying.

6. Finally, prayer for healing must be *appropriating*. Prayer reaches its climax in the appropriation of God's gifts by faith—in the reception of what God has promised. The person who prays for healing appropriates by beginning to act in the strength of the healing power being received.

By way of summary, it must be kept in mind that healing prayer is not mere conformity to a traditional pattern of prayer; rather is it an activity of faith in the One who heals. After one of my private healing services a young couple for whose child we had prayed were told by a neighbor that nothing would happen because I used the wrong procedures in prayer. After one of my public healing services, a person in the congregation remarked: "That preacher up front doesn't pray loud enough for anybody to be healed."

In both these instances the real point had been missed. Prayer is dependent not upon its format but upon its object. The issue is plain: Is the One to whom we pray able to answer prayers offered in accordance with his will? The answer is evident: God answers prayer! The Great Physician heals!

Something else should be kept in mind as we pray for healing. Prayer does not always result in immediate healing. Many times it becomes the means of guidance to an appropriate healing method. Since all healing is of God, he uses all legitimate means and methods for healing. He always cooperates with the laws of his universe and is able to bring into play even higher laws, often previously unknown to humans.

I recall in a healing mission a young couple who came to the altar as proxies for the wife's father, a prominent educator, who had suddenly been stricken with blindness. After the healing service they made their way immediately to the father's home and told him what they had done on his behalf. During the hours of that very night several members of the family became acutely conscious of an inward impression that the father should be taken to a certain opthalmologist in a well-known clinic in a distant city. This was done the following day. Later it was reported to me that the cause of the father's sudden blindness was diagnosed rather quickly, and he was beginning again to see normally.

How to Pray for One's Own Healing

Here is a suggested guide for praying for one's own healing. The format was suggested by the Rev. John H. Parke, Warden of the Order of St. Luke the Physician.

REALIZE—Know that you were born for a glorious, triumphant, and whole life, that the will of God for you is good, that the Great Physician wills wholeness for you.

REPENT—Not all illness is caused by sin, but usually somewhere, somehow, a physical or moral law of the universe has been broken, willfully or accidentally, either by you or by someone closely affecting your life. Insofar as you may have been at fault, confession and a sincere desire to change is needed.

Where another may be responsible, your forgiveness of that person is required (Mark 6:12-13; James 5:16). Put away all

99

hostility toward conditions, circumstances, persons, places, and things.

RELAX—Consciously release all the tensions of your body, all the doubts and anxieties of your mind. Lay aside all criticism, prejudices, and preconceived notions, and keep an open mind. Let go—and let God.

VISUALIZE PERFECT HEALTH—Reverse the negative patterns of disease, limitation, and troubles. Do not syndicate your ills and complaints. Using your imagination, see yourself the way you believe God wants you to be—perfect wholeness is every part of your being—body, mind, and spirit. Visualize Jesus, the Great Physician, reaching forward to touch you. As you feel his touch, know that his healing power is flowing within you.

ASK—And you shall receive (Matt. 7:7). "Whatsoever ye shall ask in my name, that will I do" (John 14:13). Ask with faith—"Lord, I believe" (Mark 9:24). "Believe that you have received it, and it will be yours" (Mark 11:24 RSV). Ask with thanksgiving—"Father, I thank thee that thou hast heard me" (John 11:41 RSV). Even before any results are evident, start thanking God that his healing power is at work. Ask with joy—"Jesus, I praise you. Jesus, I love you"—just pour out your heart in praise and love to him.

ACCEPT—Let God touch every area of your life with his power. Realize God's presence continually. Live in the now, think in the now, and act in the now. Live in a constant state of expectancy of God's constant adequacy.

DO SOMETHING IN RESPONSE TO YOUR HEALING—Do something that you could not do before. Do something for someone else who needs you. Do something special for God. Witness to all what God has done for you.[30]

How to Pray for Another's Healing

In his well-known healing volume *God Wants You to Be Well,* Laurence Blackburn gives extremely helpful suggestions about praying for another's healing:

1. Have a right relationship with the person for whom you are praying.
2. Do not judge the person for whom you are praying.
3. Try to secure the cooperation of the person for whom you are praying.
4. Pray with hope and expectation.
5. Pray for God's blessing as God may see the need.
6. Continue to pray for the person even when your prayers are resisted.
7. Pray for the person when he or she is asleep.
8. Never try to coerce or cajole God in your prayers.
9. Pray in perfect trust and with love.
10. Pray in utter honesty.
11. Pray without the fear of death.
12. Decide in advance how you are going to respond to your prayer being answered.[31]

How to Form a Healing Prayer Group

Intercessory healing prayer groups are an important part of the ministry of healing in the local church. Therefore, we need to deal with a basic question: How is a healing prayer group formed?

The immediate answer is undoubtedly a general one: A healing prayer group is formed like any other prayer group is formed. The main difference between prayer groups is not in the manner of their formation but in the focus of their spiritual activity. A healing prayer group is focused on learning to pray for healing and then praying for the healing of individuals.

The late Dr. W. E. Sangster of England, a leader in the Prayer Group Movement, gives helpful insights concerning the formation of an intercessory prayer group:

Now raise with God the question whether you should join some prayer group already in existence or start one. If you are led to start one, inquire of God to what one person you should mention the matter first. Pray further about the conversation, seek a suitable time and have an unhurried talk with that person.

Tell him or her how God has led you, why you think united prayer so important, and what you hope may come of this venture.

If—at once or after reflection—the other person agrees to join with you, you have a prayer cell. Two are enough: "Where two or three are gathered together in my name . . ." Ten or twelve might be regarded as maximum.

But how does the prayer cell of two become ten? In the same way as the one became two! Let the two pray together about whom they should ask to join. Let the invitation usually be given in private talk—one with one. Let each prospective member know what the whole idea is, how God inspired it, and how God can use it.[32]

QUESTIONS FOR REFLECTION

1. What is the nature and purpose of prayer? What does prayer mean to you?

2. Study the prayers related to some of the healing miracles of Jesus and note how they give evidence of the characteristics of healing prayer discussed in this lesson; i.e., (a) sincerity, (b) positiveness, (c) specificity, (d) anticipatory faith, (3) gratitude, and (f) appropriation.

3. Jesus talks about prayer in such scriptural passages as John 14:14; 15:7; Matthew 7:7, 11; 18:19; 21:22. How do these passages relate to prayer for healing?

4. Does the Lord's Prayer give any insights about healing prayer?

5. Are you a member of a healing prayer group? What is your healing prayer group accomplishing?

6. What have you discovered to be helps to healing prayer? Hindrances?

WHAT HINDERS HEALING?

The most frequent question I am asked in relation to healing is, Why wasn't I healed when I prayed for healing? or Why wasn't so-and-so healed as a result of an active intercessory prayer ministry on his or her behalf? Such questions compel us to face realistically the matter of so-called failures in healing and to seek to discover those factors that hinder healing.

At the outset of our probing into this area, we must keep in mind certain basic assumptions: (a) usually God does not act arbitrarily in the granting of healing power, (b) healing is not dependent upon a person's relationship to a human healer, (c) healing is in accordance with spiritual laws that we discussed in the chapter on the healing steps.

Among the myths that have developed in relation to the failure to be healed are two common misconceptions: that such a failure is sometimes the sure evidence of a lack of faith on the part of the one seeking healing and that on other occasions such failure is related to the will of God who does not purpose that a certain person be healed. We must disabuse our minds at once of these myths and the false assumptions upon which they are based.

The absence of the right kind of faith, anticipatory faith, can be a major hindrance to healing, as we shall see later in this discussion. But the lack of faith cannot be considered the sole measurement to be applied in every case of failure. The record of the healing ministry reveals that at times there are other factors that have become more causal in relation to a person's failure to be healed. Often these can be identified. Even when not identified, their influence is evident.

I think at once of several individuals on behalf of whom I have participated in active healing ministries—a missionary, a housewife, a building contractor, a teacher, a minister—and these were not healed in this life. The healing of eternity is reserved for them. But every evidence points in the direction that the failure to be healed was in no sense the result of any lack of faith on the part of any one of them. Each of them was a person of radiant, confident, persevering, hopeful faith, and each was surrounded by persons of such faith.

The second myth is also widespread—the idea that whenever a person is not healed, it must be God's intentional will that he or she not be healed. At once this assumption is seen to be diametrically opposite to the conviction that God wills wholeness for every person. A review of our previous study on "A Satisfying Theology of Healing" (chapter 5) should be helpful at this point.

The fallacy of always blaming God for the failure to be healed was dealt with meaningfully in an article from the pen of an English churchman, the Anglican Bishop of Newcastle. I quote in part:

> Why are not all healed? A possible answer would be that God was capricious in his love and blessing, and chose one and neglected another without any reason for his choice. But a capricious God is not the God revealed by Jesus Christ, nor is he the God revealed by Nature. Our Lord tells us of a divine love which is universal, going out equally to all men. Nature tells us that his actions are reasoned, orderly, and in accord with his own laws. We may rule out the idea of caprice as a principle of God's action.[33]

What then are some of the factors that may be identified as hindrances to healing? Many authors have written on the subject. One of the most illuminating discussions of this entire area is to be found in chapter 3 in the volume *God's Healing Power* by the late Edgar L. Sanford. In the list that follows, ten of the hindrances were suggested in that particular chapter. I have provided the discussion for each of these and also added another hindrance that appears as the sixth.

1. *The Negativism of the Secular World.* The prevailing climate of the secular world in which we live is one of distrust in the supernatural and doubt concerning miraculous

happenings in human experience. A sinful and faithless world exudes unhealthy spiritual air that even faithful souls must breathe. The seeker after healing must elevate his soul continually into the pure air of spirituality that transcends secular denials of the supernatural.

3. *The Negativism of the Christian World.* An even greater tragedy is the fact of negativism within the church itself. In far too many instances the contemporay church lives in a vague atmosphere of uncertain belief and dubious allegiance. Too often the individual sincerely seeking healing finds himself more or less alone, even in the midst of professing Christians. It is essential for the Christian seeking healing to keep in mind that the church that existed, historically speaking, nearest the time of Christ and that endeavored to fulfill his purpose for the church with unusual faithfulness, conducted a vital ministry of healing.

3. *The Negative Influence of Others.* A great obstacle to faith for healing is the negative influence of friends and neighbors, sometimes even members of one's own family. It is difficult for a person to become confident of God's healing power when he or she hears continually words of disbelief in relation to divine healing. One who would receive God's healing power must learn to live above the negative influence of disbelieving relatives and friends. One's entire confidence must be in God continually.

4. *Environmental Confusion.* Sometimes the very atmosphere of one's environment reacts unfavorably upon one's receptivity to spiritual blessings. If one's circumstances are characterized by restlessness, anxiety, fearfulness, and the like, it becomes increasingly difficult for the individual to escape personal distraction and tension. Such confusion impedes the flow of God's healing power.

I recall a businessman who asked me to talk with him about the possibility of a healing ministry on his behalf. When I began discussing the healing steps, beginning with the step of relaxation, he stopped me at once and remarked that there was no use continuing at the present time. He commented: "I'm engaged in a lawsuit, and I just can't take this first step of relaxation."

5. *The Absence of Proper Spiritual Motivation.* Proper spiritual motivation for healing includes a number of areas: (a) the deepest reason for wanting to be healed, (b) one's own spiritual purging as an imperative in the process of seeking healing, (c) the willingness to use all legitimate methods, including spiritual methods, in the seeking of healing, (d) the end for which the healing is to be used.

I have known individuals who had the wrong motivations in seeking healing. I remember a man who talked to me during a recess period when a ministers' conference was being held. He very bluntly said: "I want to be healed because I'm getting tired of spending all my money on doctors." He erred by acting in response to a basically commercialized motivation.

On another occasion I went to hold healing service for a lady who had been sent home from the hospital with terminal cancer. I had not met the lady before, but I knew her son. As I entered her room, filled with relatives and before I was even introduced to her, she remarked: "I'm glad you came; if it's the last thing I ever do, I'm going to show those doctors at _____ Hospital something." I knew at once her motivation was not basically spiritual, and before the healing service I tried to lead her in the proper direction for the receptivity of God's healing power.

Early in the healing steps is the step of purging. The healing of our spirits precedes the healing of our bodies and minds. We must be willing to walk in the light of Christ and be purged by his cleansing blood. It needs to be recognized that some people are not made well because they are not willing to be made whole. True healing means the purging of sin and sinful attitudes as well as the overcoming of illness and the annihilation of disease germs.

God is able to work effectively in those who cooperate with him most fully by the utilization of all the healing methods, both material and spiritual, that are available as the result of God's creation and grace. Suppose there is a known cure through physical or psychological methods. These should always be administered and utilized in the spirit of faith and prayer. Suppose there is no known cure through material methods of healing. Then all the spiritual forces released in God's universe should be called upon for direct healing. All healing is of God; he is never backed into a corner by the necessity of using only one healing method.

The highest motivation for seeking healing is that the healed person may use his recovered strength and restored wholeness for the glory of God. The prayer I use most often during the laying on of hands is this one: "Lord Jesus, heal this person for thy glory and for continuing service in thy Kingdom."

I think often of the twenty-four elders spoken of in the fourth chapter of the book of the Revelation who were each given a crown. What would you or I do if each of us received a crown? Would we keep polishing it? Would we put it away in a tarnishproof bag? Would we wear it all the time, everywhere, so that everybody would know that we had it? Would we be tempted to compare its size with other crowns, in the secret hope that it would be larger than the others?

What did the twenty-four elders do? They immediately cast their crowns before the throne and cried out: "Thou are worthy, O Lord, to receive glory and honour and power: for thou hast created all things, and for thy pleasure they are and were created." They gave their crowns back to the One who had given them in the first place. Even crowns given to humans were for the glory of God. All for Jesus! So with our healing—we give our healed selves all over again in full consecration to the One who has redeemed and healed us, that our lives may always be used in accordance with his will.

6. *The Absence of Compassion.* The healing miracles of Jesus were motivated by his compassion for people. Jesus earnestly desired that all people should experience the

wholeness that God intends. Healing power cannot flow where compassion is lacking. Both the person seeking healing and all those who participate in the healing ministry must be channels of God's redeeming and healing love. Before asking the question, Am I a healing person? ask the question, Am I a loving person?

7. *Discouragement.* No matter what its cause, the mood of discouragement is always a hindrance to healing by any means. Every effort must be made to remove the cause of discouragement. The patient must face his situation realistically and not become preoccupied with conditions beyond his control. He must free himself from tensions created by discouragement. He must discipline himself to trust in God, in relation to all things.

8. *The Absence of Anticipatory Faith.* Of all the obstacles to healing, the absence of anticipatory faith is among the most strategic. In view of the fact that it is the tendency of so-called faith healers to put all the blame right here, we must think our way clearly at this point.

Faith must be seen in its true content. It is not enough to say "I believe in God" or "I believe in a God who is all-powerful" or "I believe in a God who is able to heal." These are necessary basic steps in faith for healing, but they do not go far enough. Faith also says "I believe that God will heal; I believe that God is healing now."

Faith is the expression of a person's spirituality. Faith is the manifestation of one's highest hopes. Faith is anticipation, because of the power of God. Faith is sanctified imagination, the vision that sees oneself made whole by the healing power of God. Such faith becomes a present, power-producing, life-changing, personal reality. And as such it is essential for healing.

9. *The Continuance of the Factors That Caused the Illness in the First Place.* It is estimated that in four-fifths of the cases of illness, causes for these functional illnesses are to be found in wrong mental, emotional, and spiritual factors. Until these

negative factors that contributed to the illness in the first place are eliminated, the resulting illness will continue. For illustration, guilt can cause functional disturbances. In such cases, healing becomes impossible until the factor of guilt is resolved in a Christian manner. Or take the matter of resentment and ill will. An attitude of forgiveness is imperative before healing can take place. The same is true in regard to all the other negative emotions except the normal expression of grief.

In the purely physical areas, we cannot expect healing if we persist in violating the laws of good health. Proper nutrition, adequate exercise, and wholesome personal habits cannot be bypassed. As we know so well, we are to blame for much of our illness.

We need often to pray with Richard Wong:

> Forgive us, our Father, for our enthusiasms for the illegal and the impossible things . . . jet speeds on the crowded highways . . . private arithmetic to use on tax forms . . . and hope that pies and cakes do not add inches. So root us in the facts of life and discipline us to face the awful truths we would hide from. Amen.[34]

10. *Old Age.* The matter of aging years can present a real conflict in one's thinking about healing. Humanly speaking, it is easier to renovate a human body that is resilient with youth than a body that is wearing out with age. But spiritually speaking, it is often more natural for a mature person of older years to manifest faith in the direction of personal healing.

The issue will never be resolved fully. Suffice it to say that God's healing activity will never be limited by a person's age, if there remains work to be done by that person in order to fulfill the divine purpose. On the other hand, healing cannot be sought as a mere prolongation of life, apart from spiritual considerations.

Thus, we have discussed ten identifiable hindrances to healing. A concerned ministry of healing is aware of each of them and seeks to deal with them whenever possible. Always they must be dealt with prayerfully and humbly.

11. *Certain Unknown Factors.* But our discussion of what hinders healing would be incomplete if we did not lump together a number of unknowns. Our finiteness limits all our knowledge. We must admit that just as there lies before the medical world a vast realm of unexplored knowledge, so in the spiritual realm there are factors influencing success or failure in healing of which we are ignorant. It is our hope that some day, in our progress in the field of healing, even these factors will be made known to us. Until then we must commit even our ignorances to the wisdom of God. After all we are finite creatures, dealing with infinite power.

What About Failures in Healing?

It is often remarked that there are no failures in a ministry of healing. This is true when we keep in mind that in this life the highest healing of all is that of the human spirit and that in the world to come the resurrection of the Christian's body will provide the eternal, perfect healing. But all of us know that there are times when needed physical and psychological healings do not take place in our mortal existence. Certainly such failures do not invalidate the church's ministry of healing. If a doctor has treated a patient or a surgeon has operated on a patient who dies, he does not give up his practice. If the work of a psychiatrist fails to lead to the restoration of mental or emotional wholeness in a person, he does not throw away his profession. In the church world, the church does not stop the work of evangelism because all do not accept Jesus Christ as Savior. Nor should the church fail to engage in a healing ministry because all are not healed.

The contemporary church as the body of believers is not being true to the New Testament pattern of the church if it seeks to evade its responsibility as a healing community simply because healing does not always result. Rather should the church examine itself in the light of God's Word to see if it is in any way responsible for such failures in healing. The Bishop of Newcastle expressed this truth in these penetrating words: "Why are not all healed? God's power is limited. He has given to us the gift of free will, the power of choice; and that implies that we can help or hinder his work. Our own belief may erect a barrier which hinders the healing power of Christ from coming to them."[35]

QUESTIONS FOR REFLECTION

1. How does a person combat the negativism of the secular world, and of the religious world, in relation to healing miracles?
2. In relation to the possibility of healing, how can a person live above negative influences that are present in his or her family and social circles?
3. How does a person test his or her spiritual motivations?
4. How do you develop genuine compassion for others?
5. What are the tests of faith in relation to one's healing?
6. What is the Christian view of old age?
7. How do you react to the idea that there are no failures in a ministry of healing?

WHAT SHOULD THE CHURCH BE DOING?

Traditionally there have been various attitudes concerning the church's relationship to a ministry of healing. There are those who believe that the church should not concern itself with any ministry of healing per se. Such an attitude professes to be supported by certain philosophical and theological assumptions. The materialist claims that a person's body can be cared for by scientific means alone and thus religious help is superflous. The Bultmannian theology claims that there is no supernatural agency that can break through natural law. Some religionists believe that sickness is God's direct and disciplinary gift to men and women. Others are dispensationalists and teach that the divine gift of healing was authentic only in that particular period when the Christian church was getting started and that it has been withdrawn in subsequent dispensations.

The other extreme in attitude is found in those who declare that the church is the one true healing agency ordained of God and that it should take the place of all other healing agencies. These folks say, "Let the church do it all. Let the preacher become the doctor and surgeon. Let the worship service, the pastoral counseling session, become the dispensary, the clinic. Let there be no reliance on medical science in any of its branches. Meditation and prayers are the only true medicine. To rely upon any nonspiritual method of healing is actually distrust in divine power."

Both of the above attitudes seem to me to be unscriptural and unrealistic. In between these two extremes I discover an authentic ministry of healing for the church. The church never ceases to be under the divine mandate of the Great Commission: Go teach—go preach—go heal.

I want to express three convictions about the church and its responsibility for a healing ministry.

An Authentic Ministry

Healing is an authentic ministry of the church. I say this for at least six reasons:

First, Jesus Christ as the founder of the church inaugurated a ministry of healing. A study of the gospel records reveals that Jesus devoted much of his ministry to healing. Most of his miracles were miracles of healing. In the Gospels, there are records of at least twenty-six healing miracles that Jesus performed upon individuals. There are five other references to his healing ministry in respect to "a great multitude," "many people," and "others."

Second, the Great Commission that Jesus Christ gave to the church includes the ministry of healing. William Barclay, eminent New Testament scholar, writes: "Preaching, teaching, healing—that was the threefold pattern of the ministry of Jesus. Healing was an inseparable part of his work and of the pattern of the work of his apostles."[36]

Third, healing was a regular ministry in the early Christian church. A study of the book of the Acts and the succeeding New Testament Scriptures reveals the sixfold ministry of the early church.

1. *The Proclaiming Church* (I Cor. 1:23, 24). The good news was announced that God's Son, crucified and resurrected, had inaugurated the new Kingdom of truth, grace, and power.
2. *The Teaching Church* (Acts 2:42). Teachers were developed and trained for ministries in Jerusalem, Judea, Samaria, and the "uttermost part of the earth" (1:8).
3. *The Celebrating Church* (Rom. 15:6). With joyous praise and worship the Christians rejoiced daily that Christ was in their midst and that they were serving him.
4. *The Fellowshiping Church* (Acts 2:42). A grateful people were bound together in a close family relationship of mutual trust and ministry.

5. *The Serving Church* (Acts 2:45). A concern for the poor and a compassionate urge to share soon found expression in the organization of deacons.

6. *The Healing Church* (Acts 5:16). Sick minds and bodies were cured as the apostles were concerned about the whole person.

Fourth, healing was one of the gifts of the Spirit to the early Christian church. The apostle Paul discusses such gifts in four New Testament passages: Romans 12:6-8; I Corinthians 12:8-10; I Corinthians 12:28-30; Ephesians 4:11.

The Greek word for "gift" is *charisma,* a distinctly New Testament word that reflects the prominence of grace *(charis)* in the early church. *Charisma* is a gift of grace, a favor that one receives without any merit of his or her own.

The plural *charismata* in Pauline usage refers to effective enablings of ministry by the Holy Spirit in particular believers to serve the church of Jesus Christ. As a result of the presence of *charismata* within the lives of the members of the New Testament Church, it was equipped to perform its full-orbed ministries in the world.

In First Corinthians, Paul speaks of "diversities of gifts" (I Cor. 12:4), "differences of administrations" (v. 5), and "diversities of operations" (v. 6). There are nine gifts: the word of wisdom, the word of knowledge, the discerning of spirits, prophecy, tongues, the interpretation of tongues, faith, healing, miracles.

There are ten administrations: apostles, prophets, teachers (pastors/teachers), helps/government (administration), evangelists, ministry, exhortations, giving, ruling, showing mercy.

The nine gifts plus the ten administrations result in nineteen operations of the Spirit.

Like all the other gifts, the gift of healing was distributed in accordance with the divine wisdom (v. 11) and was to be used for the common good (v. 7). I have a deepening conviction that our concern ought not to be primarily whether certain individuals have the gift of healing but rather with the scriptural concept that healing is a gift for the church to exercise in its redemptive ministry to the needs of persons. To me it is not as important to ask the question, Do I have the gift of healing? as it is to be concerned about whether the church of which I am a part is exercising a valid healing ministry.

Fifth, the church has continued to exercise a ministry of healing through the centuries. Even though such a ministry was not as prominent during the Middle Ages as it was in the first three centuries, it continued, and no Christian century has been devoid of an authentic healing witness. The theological rediscoveries of the Protestant Reformation, while not focusing on a healing ministry as such, provided support for such a subsequent ministry of divine grace to the whole person.

Finally, there is an authentic resurgence of interest and participation in the healing ministry of the church in the contemporary age. The church is seeking to rediscover its full-orbed ministry, which, according to the New Testament, includes healing. A large number of healing books are being written, healing seminars and conferences are being attended on a large scale, an increasing number of local churches are conducting regular healing services, and everywhere there is a reawakened interest in what the church has to say and offer in this area.

A Neglected Ministry

In spite of its contemporary resurgence, healing remains largely a neglected ministry in the church. Why isn't the church more interested in a ministry of healing? I certainly do not have all the answers. But perhaps there are some insights that will help us understand better the reasons for such a neglect of a healing ministry on the part of local churches.

Let me suggest five reasons:

1. *Ignorance.* A host of ministers and lay persons are ignorant of the validity of a healing ministry in the local

church. Most ministers are the product of their training. Unfortunately, much theological training today does not include emphasis upon the full ministry of healing in the local church. The knowledge of most lay persons about the valid ministries of the church has come from their ministers. If ministers do not teach and explain and utilize the healing ministry of the church, certainly lay persons are not to be blamed for their ignorance.

On an Easter Sunday evening I conducted a mini healing seminar for a group of churches within my own Annual Conference. When I had concluded, the chairman of the meeting remarked to the congregation: "In the light of what we have heard tonight about healing, just think of all that we have failed to do through the years because we didn't know we were supposed to do it."

2. *Unbelief.* A person or an institution does not carry on an activity unless convinced of the validity of such activity. We must face the truth that many folks do not believe that the church should engage in a ministry of healing. A friend of mine who was guest preacher in a very active church in an eastern state had a copy of one of my healing booklets in his pocket. As he and the host pastor proceeded toward the pulpit, he pulled out the booklet and asked, "Do you have any objection if I mention this booklet from the pulpit today?" Quickly the host minister replied, "I don't go for that kind of thing." He just didn't believe.

Why is there much unbelief about healing in the church today? One reason is that a lack of knowledge always supports an attitude of unbelief. Truth both initiates and helps to sustain belief. Many have not investigated the historical facts about a healing ministry, revealed both in the Scriptures and in postcanonical history. They have not discovered that a healing ministry has been a part of the vital spiritual ministries of the church through the ages. Until one discovers such truth, unbelief in this area remains predominant.

For another thing, in this age of vast technological

advances, it is easy to maintain a supposed dichotomy between the spiritual and the material. How easy it is to say that it is the church's business to preach the gospel while it is given to medical science to heal the sick.

At other times, would-be believers in the church's ministry of healing have been frustrated by the appearance of evidence that seems to refute the whole idea. For illustration, a choice saint of God, fervently prayed for, is not healed. Then a person will say, "If God wants to heal a person he will; what we do about it doesn't matter. Therefore, we should limit our concerns to the things it is possible for us to accomplish."

Also we must face the fact that there are times when people stifle their belief by refusing to act. They have the evidence. They know the truth. But they will not act upon it. Certainly they need to be helped to face the reasons for their refusal to act.

3. *Prejudice.* The truth must be faced that some pastors and lay persons have become prejudiced against a healing ministry because of certain displays of spiritual arrogance and presumption in regard to it and of extreme excesses in methodology in effecting it. Some persons have made unscriptural and unsubstantiated claims for spiritual healing, and some of the results have been both caricature and casualty. Thoughtful religious leaders have often been turned off by such attitudes and activities.

I am writing these lines on a beautiful September morning. Early today on a national telecast ten minutes were devoted to a healing ministry being conducted by an ordained minister. Scene after scene was shown of persons seeking healing who became unconscious and were considered slain in the Spirit in the course of the so-called healing process. Such a presentation is certainly a distortion of the true picture of the healing ministry of the church across the centuries. It gives the false impression that healing is dependent upon some strange accompanying activity, such as being slain in the Spirit. Naturally, many religious people who are both sincere and seekers after the truth are turned off by such representations.

4. *Preoccupation.* There are those who are so preoccupied with other areas of ministry in the local church, and many of these areas are spiritually legitimate, that they have never become sensitive to the need of seeking to discover if any other valid areas of ministry are still being neglected. There are others who believe in a healing ministry but who do not know how to fit anything more into their already overloaded pastoral schedules and church programs.

5. *The high cost of a healing ministry.* It costs something to have a healing ministry. There are the high costs of overcoming the fear of failure, of daring to go out on a limb for Christ, of developing an ever-deepening Christian compassion, of submitting to the demanding personal spiritual disciplines required, of accepting any stigmas that may result, of depending totally upon the Holy Spirit.

In June, 1977, there appeared in *The United Church Observer,* the official periodical of the United Church of Canada, an article entitled "Healing in the United Church? Why Not?" The author relates how he first thought seriously about a healing ministry during his days in seminary, but then failed to do anything about it during the early years of his full-time ministry. Why? Hear his own words:

> I was first taught the scriptural basis for this ministry during post-graduate study almost ten years ago. Fear kept me from using it—fear of committing myself to something few of my colleagues were engaged in, fear of misunderstanding, opposition, division.

Most of the article is devoted to a description of the dynamic healing ministry now being conducted in the author's church. Things began to happen as soon as he was willing to pay the price for such a healing ministry.

A Needed Ministry

Healing should become a regular ministry in the local church. How can this be realized? What steps will make this possible? Let me offer some suggestions about making healing a vital ministry in the local church:

1. The spiritual leaders within the local congregation—the pastor in cooperation with concerned lay persons—must be willing to initiate and then carry forward a healing ministry. Such action is taken in response to a growing awareness of the extensive need for healing that exists in every congregation.

2. The local congregation must rediscover the concept of the church as a healing community. The New Testament church was a healing community. The periods in church history when the church has been the most vital have been those when the church ministered most faithfully to the wholeness of persons and of society.

Hobart Mowrer writes: "A religious congregation, worthy of the name, ought to be a 'therapeutic community': but . . . most religious groups have little or no redemptive potency."[37]

The healing ministry is the responsibility of the total Christian community. James C. McGilvray, director of the Christian Medical Council, commenting on the affirmations of the Tubingen Healing Conference in 1964, writes:

> The healing role is given to the congregation, the People of God, who must exercise this dimension of their calling to the sick world in which they live. This dimension of the church's life has to a great extent been lost by relegating it to those who are professionally trained. . . . Man and his society cry out for healing and for wholeness, and where else will they find them but in the therapeutic community which is or should be the church? . . . It is too romantic to consider the church as a "community of healing" if only physical healing is involved. The church is a "community of healing" in relation to the total concept of "salvation and health."[38]

3. A local congregation must be helped to appreciate the contributions of a healing ministry to the life of the church. A study report from the United Church of Christ listed the following contributions that the modern healing movement

have made to the church: (a) quickened concern for the individual, (b) more intimate focus upon the nearness of God, (c) something always happens as a result of prayer, (d) new interest in spiritual resources, (e) increased participation of the worshiper, (f) the whole person is served, (g) prevention of illness.

Wherever there has been a vital healing ministry, a local church has experienced spiritual renewal. A young pastor shared with me some exciting spiritual news about his church. He related that he prepared a series of sermons on the six healing steps that we have already studied. He commented that he felt his church needed to be healed corporately as much as any person in it needed to be healed individually.

His first sermon was on the church's need of reverent relaxation in the holy presence of God. He then preached on the church's need of purging by the Blood of Christ. The third sermon was an analysis of the evident needs of that particular congregation. When he preached his fourth sermon on consecration, a revival broke out in his church. His congregation began to be healed as a corporate community. (Both of us were so excited about the revival in the congregation that I failed to find out whether he went ahead and preached on the last two healing steps.)

4. The local church should take advantage of the various opportunities afforded for a healing ministry. The church is a healing community. The opportunities for an authentic healing ministry are manifold:

   a. The church should teach and preach the gospel of health and healing.

   b. The church should cooperate with all other legitimate agencies of healing in the community.

   c. The church should provide worship and fellowship opportunities that are genuinely therapeutic in their effects.

   d. The church should maintain a vital revival and evangelism program. The deepest of all healing is that of the soul in its relationship to God and to others. Such spiritual healing often results in healing in other areas of the person's life.

e. The church should utilize the healing power of the sacraments.

f. The church should sponsor active prayer groups that exercise continuing intercessory ministry for the healing of persons.

g. The church should conduct regular healing services. (These will be discussed in detail in the next chapter.)

h. The church should provide continuing opportunities for healing counseling.

i. The church should carry on a ministry of reconciliation between alienated persons and groups.

Every church must face conscientiously what it ought to be doing in relation to a healing ministry. A West Coast newspaperwoman chanced to see inscribed on the cornerstone of a fashionable church in New York City the instructions Jesus gave his followers: "Heal the sick, cleanse the lepers, raise the dead, cast out devils." On the impulse of the moment, she walked around to the rectory door and asked to see the rector.

"I saw your sign," she stated abruptly without any further explanation. "Do you?"

"My sign? Do I what?" asked the bewildered cleric.

"Are you doing what your sign says? Do you heal the sick, cleanse the lepers, raise the dead, cast out demons?" Then, without waiting for the astonished minister to reply, she continued, "If you don't you shouldn't advertise."

QUESTIONS FOR REFLECTION

1. How do you evaluate your local church in relation to the following ministries?
   a. Preaching the gospel
   b. Teaching the Scriptures
   c. Worshiping reverently
   d. Enjoying spiritual fellowship
   e. Meeting the needs of the people it serves
   f. Carrying on a healing ministry
2. How do you react to the idea that perhaps in our day the gift of healing is given primarily to the Christian community?
3. How can you help a church member who (a) doesn't believe in the healing ministry or (b) who is prejudiced against the healing ministry or (c) who says he or she doesn't have time for the healing ministry?
4. How can we correct false images of the healing ministry that are often presented through the media?
5. Emily Gardiner Neal says that the healing ministry of the church is one of the chief evidences that Christ is alive today. Do you agree?
6. Does gospel preaching include talking about health and healing?

HOW TO BEGIN A MINISTRY OF HEALING IN A LOCAL CHURCH

It has been remarked repeatedly that the contemporary church is experiencing a genuine revival of the healing ministry. Some years ago Cyril Richardson spoke prophetically in this regard: "There can be no question that primitive Christianity was among other things a healing cult. . . . We see today a revival of this concern of the primitive church for the healing of the sick." He further felt that this movement "is to be welcomed in recalling us to forgotten truths and some neglected power of the church."

In the last chapter we noted the many ways in which the local church can participate in a ministry of healing. Among the several things we discussed are the church's opportunity and responsibility to sponsor such specialized ministries as intercessory healing prayer groups and regular healing services. This chapter is an attempt to give practical guidance to concerned persons in a local church as to how to proceed to make specialized healing ministries a part of the continuing program of the church.

As you read this chapter you will undoubtedly get the impression that the material is aimed primarily at the minister. It is assumed that the pastor of the church will take the lead in establishing a ministry of healing in a local church. Nevertheless, it will be impossible for any pastor to do this effectively without the full cooperation of concerned lay persons. Therefore, it is also assumed that the material in this chapter will be helpful to lay persons who want to assist in inaugurating a ministry of healing in their local churches. Interested lay persons should seek to discover all the ways to be participants in such an undertaking.

Let me offer my suggestions under five general headings for beginning a ministry of healing in a local church:

Conviction

The pastor and cooperating lay persons must become convinced of the validity of a ministry of healing in a local church. There are various areas of study that will aid in the growth of such a conviction: (a) an understanding of the meaning of healing, (b) a recognition of the biblical basis for a healing ministry, (c) an adequate theology of healing, (d) the facing of the fact that most contemporary persons desperately need some kind of healing, and (e) a deepening awareness that a loving, redeeming God has made provision for wholeness.

Communication

The pastor who is becoming increasingly convinced of the validity of a healing ministry and who desires to inaugurate such a healing ministry must participate in effective communication with his people concerning the important truths in this spiritual realm that are emerging in his mind and heart.

There are several natural ways in which pastors can communicate effectively with their people concerning their growing convictions in the area of healing. They can speak of them in appropriate counseling sessions and pastoral visitations upon the sick. They can let illustrations in their sermons, from time to time, bear testimony to the reality of healing. In midweek Bible studies, they can occasionally give a series that includes the miracles of Jesus. And when discussing the healing miracles, they should emphasize their literal healing aspects as well as their spiritual lessons. How prone we are, in speaking of the miracles, to talk in a vein like this: "The miracle of Jesus healing a blind man means that Jesus is able to open the blind eyes of a man's sinful soul" or "The miracle of healing the impotent man at the pool means that Jesus is able to make a man spiritually sound." Should there not be occasions when we are confident to say also that Jesus healing a blind man means that he is able to give sight to blind eyes and that Jesus healing an impotent man means that he is able to restore wholeness to a person's body.

The pastor will reach a climax in his communication with his people when he presents a series of sermons on healing from his pulpit. These sermons should be the homiletical embodiment of his convictions. The truth concerning healing should be presented clearly and persuasively. And it would be helpful if a period of questions and discussion could be held between the sermons in the series.

Just so, the concerned lay person can participate effectively in this entire process of communication. As the lay person continues studying and becomes increasingly convinced, there are innumerable ways for sharing such conviction with others—in private conversations, in sharing in prayer and Bible study groups, in personal witnessing, in Sunday school class discussions, and in periods of family devotions. Certainly a Sunday school teacher has an unexcelled opportunity to communicate convictions through the prepared lessons and in personal contacts with members of the class.

Commencement

There will come an opportune time for the beginning of a healing ministry in the local church. Perhaps the earliest form of this will be expressed in the formation of prayer groups, whose chief purpose will be that of intercessory prayer for healing. Or perhaps the healing ministry will commence with the holding of regular healing services.

Let me share my own experience in relation to healing services. There is a divergence of opinion about whether such services should be public. I am convinced that they should be. For many years, in my local church, I held such a public healing service once a month at a regularly stated time.

Even though the healing service would be open to the public, I think that only those individuals seriously interested in the relation between religion and healing should be urged to attend. The healing service should be conducted in a place that is suitable for meditation and devotion, and during the healing service ample opportunity should be given for such personal meditation.

Here is the general format I used for the healing services in my church:

PERIOD OF PRIVATE MEDITATION AND PRAYER
(Focusing attention upon the healing Christ)

SCRIPTURE (The reading of one of the healing miracles of Jesus Christ)

PRAYER   By leader.

TESTIMONIES TO HEALINGS   By those present.

BRIEF MESSAGE (not more than five minutes)   By the leader on some phase of the healing ministry (the field is unlimited—scriptural incidents, the laws of health, the principles of healing, contemporary testimonies to healing, questions that have been asked about healing, etc.).

PRAYERS FOR THE HEALING OF THOSE PRESENT AND THE LAYING ON OF HANDS

For the period of prayer for the healing of those present, those interested in receiving such healing for themselves should be invited to come forward, with bared head, and kneel at an altar rail. Then together the supplicants could pray such a prayer as this:

Lord, I know that thou canst heal me. Fill me at this moment with thyself. Let every part of me—body, mind, spirit—be filled with new life, for thou art life. Cleanse and forgive me of all sin and make me whole. Heal me so that I may be an instrument of love in thy service. Amen.

Then could follow the laying on of hands by the minister, accompanied by a brief prayer for healing for each person individually.

BENEDICTION

After the laying on of hands and before the benediction, if time permits, it is in order to have a PERIOD OF INTERCESSION during which those in attendance would be asked to intercede personally and collectively for those persons not present who are known to be in need of definite healing and for whom prayer is requested.

Here are some suggestions for brief meditations which I have used at healing services:

What Jesus Said to Those Who Sought His Healing
1. "Wilt thou be made whole?" John 5:6
2. "Believe ye that I am able to do this?" Matt. 9:28
3. "According to your faith be it unto you." Matt. 9:29
4. "Thou art made whole: sin no more." John 5:14

The Responsibility Is Yours (Use J. B. Phillips' translation of Mark 9:14-29).
1. "If you can do anything."
2. "If *I* can do anything."
3. "Everything is possible to the man who believes."

The Holy Spirit Quickens the Human Body (Rom. 8:11)
1. When we have the Holy Spirit we have the power of God that effected the resurrection of Jesus Christ.
2. This same power that effected the resurrection of Jesus Christ from the dead is able to heal our mortal bodies.

The Healing of the Nobleman's Son (John 4:43-54)
1. The highest faith does not require a sign, but the highest faith always effects those things that become signs.
2. The healing was effected "at the same hour"—
   when the nobleman believed without a sign;
   when Jesus said: "Thy son liveth."

The Blind Man of Bethsaida (Mark 8:22-26)
1. Concerned persons bring others to Christ for healing.
2. Jesus Christ is always interested in human need.
3. When Jesus Christ begins a healing work he always carries it through to a successful completion.

Here is another order of worship for a healing service in a local church. It is patterned after the service developed by

Alfred W. Price, International Warden of the Order of St. Luke the Physician, while he was serving as rector of St. Stephen's P. E. Church, Philadelphia.

THE INVITATION

It is vitally important to bear in mind that the whole ministry of healing is possible only through the person of our Lord Jesus Christ. He is the One who heals. The human disciple, whether minister or lay person, has not power of his or her own to heal. Only the Master of life can do that.

Jesus healed everyone who came to him in faith, believing, and he who is the "same yesterday, to-day, and for ever" continues to pour out his blessing of health as we are able to receive it. If we bring only a small vessel of faith to him, he will fill it, but if our vessel is large, he will fill it with equal readiness.

He who gives the laying on of hands does so only in the name of Christ. As you kneel, you are coming to him, for the human agent is only the instrument that God uses to fill sick spirits and minds and bodies with his health and wholeness.

As you come, let not your mind dwell upon your problem or on the problem of those for whom you wish to intercede. Nor let your thoughts be those of fear, resentment, or anxiety. Rather meditate upon the love of God, his willingness to forgive, his eagerness to heal, and his power to make all things new. Come in simple faith, knowing that Christ, the Great Physician, is here to bless.

Finally, before departing, thank him for the healing power that is flowing through you now. Even before there is any tangible evidence, repeat Jesus' own words: "I thank thee, Father, that thou hearest me always." Know in your own heart that God's healthful powers have been, and are being, released in you. "Lord, I thank thee" is your humble acknowledgement that healing is taking place.

OPENING SENTENCES

Hear what our Lord Jesus Christ saith, "Heal the sick . . .

and say unto them, The kingdom of God is come nigh unto you. What things ye desire when ye pray, believe that ye receive them, and ye shall have them."

Hear also what James saith, "Is any sick among you? let him call for the elders of the church; and let them pray over him, anointing him with oil in the name of the Lord. And the prayer of faith shall save the sick, and the Lord shall raise him up; and if he has committed sins, they shall be forgiven him."

And Paul writes: "Be ye transformed by the renewing of your mind. God hath not given us the spirit of fear; but of power, and of love, and of a sound mind."

"Seeing that we have a great high priest, that is passed into the heavens, Jesus, the Son of God. Let us therefore come boldly unto the throne of grace, that we may obtain mercy, and find grace to help in time of need."

A HYMN

THE SERVICE OF HOLY COMMUNION

A SCRIPTURE LESSON

A MEDITATION ON SCRIPTURE

A PERIOD OF INTERCESSION:

Minister: Jesus said, "What things soever ye desire, when ye pray, believe that ye receive them, and ye shall have them." Let us humbly and gratefully accept his forgiveness and healing, and in this confidence pray for our own needs and the needs of others.

Minister: The Lord be with you.

Response: **And with thy spirit.**

Minister: Let us lift our prayers to God for those in need, speaking audibly the first names of those for whom we intercede.

(SILENT PRAYER)

Minister: Almighty God, our heavenly Father, we bring into thy healing presence all who are in need, particularly those who have asked for our prayers, in the sure confidence that thy will for them is perfect wholeness. May they find that union with the healing Christ that is the way to the Father's Presence and that will enable the full measure of thy healing power to flow into them. May they be restored to soundness of health and cheerfulness of mind, that they may rise up to serve thee with thankful hearts, through thy Son Jesus Christ, who came that we might have life and have it more abundantly. Amen.

Our Father, we beseech thee to bless all doctors, nurses, hospital chaplains, and all who seek for the healing of the sick. Give them sympathy, skill, knowledge and faith, tenderness and patience. We pray thee to bless all hospitals, convalescent and healing homes, and all sanctuaries of healing. May all means being used for the recovery of the sick be recognized as gifts from thee, and may they be used for thy glory as instruments of thy healing power, through thy Son Jesus Christ who came to save and to heal. Amen.

THE LAYING ON OF HANDS

All who wish to receive the laying on of hands for the forgiveness of sins; for the healing of mind, body, or spirit; or for strength for a personal problem, are invited to come to the altar rail. If it is difficult to kneel, you may be seated on the front pew. You may come for yourself or as a proxy for others, but as you come, come to Christ who has power to heal all our diseases and to meet our every need.

A PRAYER OF THANKSGIVING
A HYMN OF PRAISE
THE BENEDICTION

Public healing services can be conducted on a high spiritual level. They offer spiritual inspiration to those in attendance, and they result in definite healing blessings and acts.

Counseling

A ministry of healing in a local church must be undergirded by enlightened and sustained counseling. People must be helped to understand the difference between imagined and real sickness and how to deal with each. There is a sense of urgency here because imagined sickness soon becomes real sickness if not dealt with properly. People who are really sick must be aided in understanding the true nature of their sicknesses and in diagnosing the causes. In cases of physical and psychological illnesses, people must be directed to the most effective healing agencies. The work of the minister in a healing ministry always requires dedicated skill in the matter of necessary referrals to others.

In those cases where people will be seeking definite healing through the church's ministry of healing, they must be counseled carefully in the healing steps and thus be prepared for the laying on of hands at a healing service.

There must be counseling concerning the meaning of faith and the nature of prayer in healing. After healing services there is usually the need for clear communication concerning the barriers to healing.

Because of the imperative of counseling in the healing ministry of a local church, I am convinced that the time and effort and concern involved is one of the major items in the high cost of a healing ministry.

Continuity

Once a healing ministry is inaugurated in a local church, it should be carried on with dedicated regularity. I believe that such a healing ministry should remain at all times under the spiritual leadership of the pastor. This does not minimize the spiritual significance of lay persons in such a healing ministry. It only guarantees a continuity in leadership that will result in growth and enlarged spiritual effectiveness.

Jesus Christ has commissioned his church to a ministry of healing. His words, "Go—preach, teach, heal," have timeless relevance. And whenever the church engages in a ministry of healing in accordance with the objective and principles of such a ministry as outlined in the New Testament, spiritual renewal results, and the local congregation identifies itself clearly as a member of the Body of Christ.

QUESTIONS FOR REFLECTION

1. How would you respond if your minister asked you to help inaugurate a ministry of healing in your local church?

2. Should a lay person suggest to a minister that he or she should begin a healing ministry in the church? If so, what should be the approach?

3. What can lay persons do to help the minister who is active in a healing ministry carry his heavy load of healing counseling?

4. How can the minister and the lay person cooperate in the continuance of a healing ministry in the local church?

5. When a minister who has had an active healing ministry moves to another church, what is the responsibility of lay persons who are concerned about the continuance of the healing ministry in relation to the new pastor?

6. When a minister who has had an active healing ministry moves to a church that does not have such a ministry, how should that minister proceed to carry on a healing ministry?

WHAT SHALL I DO?

Even though I do not presume to be a prophet in the technical sense of the word, I would venture some predictions about future trends in the healing ministry of the church.

1. The healing ministry of the church will continue to grow and expand rapidly. It will find continually enlarged expressions in spiritually sensitive congregations. It will aid greatly in the recovery of the prophetic and priestly ministries of the church. It will contribute significantly to the continuing renewal of the church.

2. The growing healing ministry of the church will demand a deepening understanding of the true nature of prayer. Healing flows in response to prayer. But prayer must be practiced at its deepest levels and its widest ranges. Healing prayer requires far more than mere "now I lay me down to sleep" content or prayers that are continually focused on "give me." In our praying for healing we must advance through the stages of "show me" and "make me," and arrive at the level of "use me." This much higher stage is true intercession, when a person is so aligned with the purposes of God that he or she becomes the channel of God's healing power to others.

3. There will be increasing explorations into the full extent of the healing power of Jesus Christ. Vast strategic areas beckon us forward. The healing power of Christ must be related more intimately to the needs of the human spirit. Insensitive, indifferent, contemporary man must be restored to sensitive, meaningful relations to God and to his fellows. Much progress needs to be made in relation to the healing of the emotions. How can a person really be healed of his self-centeredness? How can hate be turned into love?

What about the healing of alcoholics and addicts of other drugs? What about the healing of homosexuals and those persons who seek to change their God-given sexual nature?

What about the healing of every form of sexual deviation and perversion? Certainly the healing power of Christ must be discovered as relevant in all these areas.

The healing power of Christ must also be explored in relation to every known physical ill. For illustration, the healing of cancer is more than a scientific challenge; it is also an opportunity in the realm of the spirit. In the days ahead, along with increasing medical research into the cause of cancer there must also be much more intensive research on the part of those engaged in the healing ministry of the church.

4. There will be a growing cooperation between doctors and church members—clergy and laity—in relation to healing. Much progress has already been made in this area. The medical profession is dedicated to the medicine of the person. It is becoming increasingly aware of the relation between faith and healing. The medical profession seems to have an increasing appreciation of spiritual methods of healing. There are innumerable illustrations of healing teams of doctors and clergy at work today. Certainly much more will be done in this strategic area in the years just ahead.

The healing ministry is becoming increasingly active in the contemporary church. Healing activities will become even more prominent in the years ahead. Therefore, every person who is convinced of the validity of the healing ministry of the church and who wants to be a part of it, faces an exceedingly personal question: What shall I do?

Each of us can do a number of things. For one thing, I can help dispel the myths about healing that are often voiced in the Christian world. Here is a list of myths about healing that are false, and each of us has a responsibility to refute them through healing truth:

—The only sicknesses Jesus healed were psychosomatic.
—The Divine Commission to heal has been withdrawn from the church.
—The church today has no business talking about the gospel of health or the gospel of healing.

—Salvation and wholeness are not necessarily related; it is possible to save a soul without saving a person.

—The healing ministry is restricted to physical healing.

—Healing is always an instantaneous dramatic act and not usually a process.

—Healing is achieved through magical methods or merely humanistic gimmicks.

—Healing is a haphazard happening, unrelated to laws and orderly processes.

—The failure to be healed is due solely to a person's lack of faith.

—The use of material means and methods in healing is a denial of faith.

—A person has no personal responsibility in the process of healing.

—Satan can effect genuine healing.

—The gift of healing is so indissolubly linked with another special spiritual gift that one is dependent upon the other.

—A person's healing can be complete without the basic healing of one's spirit.

—It doesn't make any difference what a person does with his or her healing.

—The healing ministry is not authentic unless everyone is healed.

—Healing means deathlessness.

—The exercise of the healing ministry is limited to a few selected individuals rather than to the church as a whole.

What shall I do? I can recognize that every Christian is called by God to be a minister of healing and thus exercise a personal ministry of healing. Everyone who has experienced the healing power of the risen Christ and whose heart is set on fire by the Holy Ghost is already in his ministry. Every Christian has a healing ministry. Each of us, regardless of calling, has a role in the healing community. In a real sense the ministry of healing is a part of the universal priesthood of all believers.

The healing ministry is not merely the exercise of a gift we possess but the practice of a capacity that we develop. It is the capacity to receive and transmit the healing grace and power of God. Such a capacity is developed under the inspiration of the Holy Spirit in response to one's total surrender to the Spirit. When one surrenders totally, the Holy Spirit pardons, cleanses, and empowers. But the development of such a spiritual capacity also is the result of regular devotional periods in the presence of Christ, during which there is practiced increasingly the consciousness of the divine presence and power. Those who develop and exercise such a capacity continue to be receiving and transmitting instruments of divine healing power.

Paul Tournier reminds us: "We are called, then, to exercise around us this ministry of soul-healing, to interest ourselves in others and in their deepest preoccupations, to listen to them with love, to make our witness before them, to uphold them with our faith, and to pray."[39]

What shall I do? I can also experience the healing power of God in my own life as my daily strength and on those occasions when I have special needs for personal healing in any of the areas of my life. Having experienced the healing power of Christ myself, I will be an authentic witness when I testify to others of the availability of divine power for their needs. This is the New Testament model for ministry in every area: being "a witness both of these things which thou hast seen, and of those things in which I will appear unto thee" (Acts 26:16).

What shall I do? I can participate wholeheartedly in the healing ministry of my church. Perhaps some of us will be privileged to participate in such a ministry in its inaugural states. Certainly we will want to participate wholeheartedly in a healing ministry as it is carried on with regularity. Actually, to encourage such participation in the healing ministry of the church has been a major purpose of this entire book. May God grant that all of us will be fashioned into God's healing community and that we will be increasingly used by God in helping to restore wholeness to persons all about us.

QUESTIONS FOR REFLECTION

1. How has your thinking about healing changed as a result of this book? How have these changes influenced (a) your theology, (b) your spiritual life, (c) your practice of prayer, (d) your ministries in the church?

2. Do you have remaining myths about healing that need to be dispelled? Identify them. Discuss them with others, in the light of the content of this book and of other healing writings with which you are familiar.

3. Write out your personal convictions about healing. List only the things that you believe confidently. Are your positive convictions about healing adequate to support you in an active ministry of healing in your church?

4. Now identify any doubts that you may still have in relation to healing. Are you willing to deal with them and seek to resolve them? If so, how will you do it?

5. Whom have you met today who needed some kind of healing? What kind of healing? Were you able to be a minister of healing to that person?

6. Are you willing at all times to be one through whom Christ heals?

NOTES

1. Bernard Martin, *Healing for You,* trans. A. A. Jones (Richmond: John Knox Press, 1966), p. 153.
2. James D. Van Buskirk, *Religion, Healing and Health* (New York: Macmillan, 1952), p. 94.
3. T. F. Davey, "The Healing Ministry in the Mission of the Church," *For Health and Healing,* November-December, 1965, p. 169.
4. Leslie D. Weatherhead, *Psychology, Religion, and Healing,* rev. ed. (Nashville: Abingdon, 1952), p. 464.
5. Morton T. Kelsey, *Healing and Christianity* (New York: Harper, 1973), p. 307.
6. Van Buskirk, *Religion, Healing and Health,* pp. 121-49.
7. Paul Sangster, *Pity My Simplicity* (London, Epworth Press, 1963), p. 154.
8. E. Stanley Jones, *The Way* (Nashville: Abingdon, 1946), p. 255.
9. Addison H. Leitch, *Interpreting Basic Theology* (New York: Hawthorne Books, 1961), pp. 53-59.
10. Paul Tournier, *The Person Reborn* (New York: Harper, 1966), p. 75.
11. Frank G. Slaughter, *Medicine for Moderns* (New York: Messner, 1947), p. 11.
12. Laurence H. Blackburn, *God Wants You to Be Well* (New York: Morehouse-Barlow, 1970), p. 67.
13. William E. Hocking, *Human Nature and Its Remaking,* rev. ed. (New York: AMS Press, 1976), p. 279.
14. Robert B. Reeves, Jr., *Union Seminary Review,* Winter, 1969, p. 196.
15. Ernest White, *The Way of Release* (Fort Washington, Penn.: Christian Literature Crusade, 1960), p. 11.
16. Van Buskirk, *Religion, Healing and Health,* p. 94.
17. Paul Tournier, *A Place for You* (New York: Harper, 1968), p. 189.
18. Blackburn, *God Wants You to Be Well,* p. 154.
19. John Birkbeck, ed., *A Thought for Every Day from Henry Drummond* (Old Tappan, N. J.: Fleming H. Revell, 1973), p. 82.
20. *Ibid.,* p. 24.
21. Jim Glennon, "The Ministry of Healing of St. Andrew's Cathedral" (newsletter), September 27, 1972.
22. Blackburn, *God Wants You to Be Well,* pp. 139-54.
23. Jones, *The Way,* pp. 260-63.
24. George Nakajima, "The Third Prayer," *The Herald,* April 15, 1964, p. 24.
25. Dorothy Davis, "The Only Explanation Is God," in *ibid.,* July 20, 1966, p. 24.
26. E. Stanley Jones, *A Song of Ascents: A Spiritual Autobiography* (Nashville: Abingdon, 1968), pp. 89-90.
27. *Ibid.,* pp. 339-40.
28. E. Stanley Jones, *Growing Spiritually* (Nashville: Abingdon, 1953), p. 293.
29. Alexis Carrel, *Reader's Digest,* March, 1941. "Prayer Is Power," pp. 34-36.

30. John H. Parke, "How to Pray for Healing," *Sharing Magazine,* July, 1973, pp. 16-17.

31. Blackburn, *God Wants You to Be Well,* chap. 9.

32. W. E. Sangster, *Teach Me to Pray* (Nashville: Upper Room, 1959), p. 9.

33. Bishop of Newcastle, "Why Are Not All Healed?" *Sharing Magazine,* December, 1962, p. 3.

34. Richard Wong, *Prayers from an Island* (Richmond: John Knox Press, 1968).

35. Bishop of Newcastle, "Why Are Not All Healed?" p. 3.

36. William Barclay, *The Mind of Jesus* (New York: Harper, 1961), p. 67.

37. O. Hobart Mowrer, *The New Group Therapy* (New York: Van Nostrand, 1964), pp. iv-v.

38. James C. McGilvray, "A Review of Christian Medical Work Today," *International Review of Missions,* April, 1968, p. 213-16.

39. Tournier, *The Person Reborn,* p. 229.

BIBLIOGRAPHY

Beard, Rebecca. *Everyman's Goal*. Evesham, England: Arthur James, 1963.
——. *Everyman's Mission*. Arthur James, 1969.
——. *Everyman's Search*. Arthur James, 1962.
Blackburn, Laurence H. *God Wants You to Be Well*. New York: Morehouse-Barlow, 1970.
Blanton, Smiley and Norman V. Peale. *Faith Is the Answer*. Tadworth, England: World's Work, 1957.
Cramer, Raymond L. *The Psychology of Jesus and Mental Health*. Los Angeles: Robert G. Cowan, 1959.
Frazier, Claude A., comp. *Faith Healing: Finger of God? or Scientific Curiosity?* Camden, N. J.: Thomas Nelson, 1973.
Kelsey, Morton T. *Healing and Christianity*. New York: Harper, 1973.
Mandus, Brother. *The Divine Awakening*. Evesham, England: Arthur James, 1961.
MacNutt, Francis. *Healing*. Notre Dame, Ind.: Ave Maria Press, 1974.
McMillen, S. I. *None of These Diseases*. Old Tappan, N. J.: Fleming H. Revell, 1963.
Neal, Emily G. *A Reporter Finds God Through Spiritual Healing*. New York: Morehouse-Barlow, 1965.
——. *The Lord Is Our Healer*. Chadwell Heath, England: L. N. Fowler & Co., 1963.
——. *The Healing Power of Christ*. London: Hodder & Stoughton, 1972.
Parker, William and Elaine St. Johns. *Prayer Can Change Your Life*. Englewood Cliffs, N. J.: Prentice-Hall, 1957.
Parkhurst, Genevieve. *Healing and Wholeness*. Rev. ed. Evesham, England: Arthur James, 1965.
Pitts, John. *Divine Healing: Fact or Fiction*. Evesham, England: Arthur James, 1962.
Price, Alfred W. *Ambassadors of God's Healing*. Philadelphia, Penn.: St. Stephan's Episcopal Church.
Sanford, Agnes. *Behold Your God*. Evesham, England: Arthur James, 1961.
——. *The Healing Gifts of the Spirit*. Arthur James, 1966.
——. *The Healing Light*. Arthur James, 1963.
Scharlemann, Martin H. *Healing and Redemption*. St. Louis: Concordia, 1965.
Simpson, A. B. *The Gospel of Healing,* Harrisburg, Penn.: Christian Publications, 1915.
Tournier, Paul. *The Healing of Persons*. New York: Harper, 1965.
——. *The Person Reborn*. Harper, 1966.
——. *The Whole Person in a Broken World*. Harper, 1964.
——. *A Doctor's Casebook in the Light of the Bible*. Harper, 1960.
——. *The Meaning of Persons*. Harper, 1957.

————. *A Place for You.* Harper, 1968.

Weatherhead, Leslie D. *Psychology, Religion, and Healing.* Nashville: Abingdon, 1954.

White, Anne S. *Healing Adventure.* Evesham, England: Arthur James, 1969.

NOTE: For a more extensive bibliography on healing, a theological library should be consulted. (The Alfred W. Price Healing Collection is located in the B. L. Fisher Library, Asbury Theological Seminary, Wilmore, Kentucky.)